HUMANITY 2.0

Book 1 *"The New Humanity"* Series
on the Spiritual Awakening of Humanity

Second Edition
The New Humanity

Charol Messenger

HUMANITY 2.0

Book 1 "The New Humanity" Series
on the Spiritual Awakening of Humanity

Second Edition

Copyright © 2012-2018 by Charol Messenger

ISBN-13: **978-1-7320717-4-2**
Library of Congress Control Number: 2011914044

February 28, 2018 SECOND EDITION includes new Bowker ISBN, 2016 Second Place International Book Excellence Book Award (sole finalist in spirituality), two National Finalist Awards, and Third Place EVVY Award. Plus many reviews, new book description and author bio. Also, modified format; and Vol. II updated, rewritten, rearranged, and condensed to reduce page volume.

Messenger Publishing
The New Humanity Author
Denver, Colorado thenewhumanityauthor.com
charolmessenger.com CharolM@aol.com

CreateSpace.com/**8192972** Plus IngramSpark and more.

Cover photo: "Human figure emerges from light," ID: 270828611 © Bruce Rolff, release Shutterstock, Inc. standard license.

Volume I © 1994, 2000, 2001 as *The New Humanity* (all previous versions discontinued), Third Place Winner 2002 CIPA EVVY Awards. Volume II © 2011-2018.

International Second Place Winner!
Book Excellence Awards 2016
(sole Finalist) in Spirituality

National Finalist USA Best Books, New Age Nonfiction 2012

Finalist CIPA EVVY Awards, Spirituality 2012

Third Place CIPA EVVY, Spirituality 2002
for First Edition, *The New Humanity* (Vol. I)

Vol. I — four chapters published in *Celestine Connection* quarterly newsletter, Denver CO

Vol. I — four other chapters published in *The Oracle Times* newsletter, Washington state

As seen at
2018 INATS Trade Show Denver
2018 ALA Mid-Winter Book Show Denver
2017 Frankfurt, Germany International Book Fair

"Wow!" ~ *The Futurist,* World Future Society

"Uplifting. Inspirational." ~ Bud Gardner

"New enlightening concepts."
~ Midwest Book Review

Rick Doksai, senior editor, *The Futurist,* World Future Society, www.wfs.org/futurist-interviews: "I was wowed by it, personally... profoundly spiritual... does touch on a lot of themes that are very relevant to the World Future Society.... another voice of hope for progress... In *Humanity 2.0,* Messenger describes a new evolutionary stage for the human species that she says is now under way: Communication networks are flourishing, cultural barriers are breaking down, and individuals everywhere are attaining new levels of empathy, insight, and awareness."

MIDWEST BOOK REVIEW, D. Donovan, Senior Reviewer: "New age, spirituality, and science too seldom cross paths - or, if they do, they tend to head in opposite directions entirely, with conclusions that don't connect. For something different - and an approach that requires an open mind of scientist readers and new age thinkers alike - take a look at *Humanity 2.0.*

"Here is a wide-ranging discussion that includes: DNA, the cosmos, angels, messengers, evolution, psychology, energy sources in the universe, and visionary thinking. And, by the way: the latter is a key to appreciating just how vast and all-embracing is the universe of *Humanity 2.0.*

"Readers can anticipate a whirlwind of ideas, and should be prepared to give this book a lot of time; not just for reading, but for absorbing many new, enlightening concepts.

"From how to recognize and use options provided by the universe to how to acknowledge the presence, effects and purposes of synchronicity in one's life, why the human species as a whole is transcending (and into what), and how personal growth insights and opportunity are linked into this process, Messenger uses posts from her meditations and angel encounters to get her point across.

"If this all seems ethereal and new age - it is. If it seems to hold a high level of transcendent thinking in and of itself - well, don't expect easy reading, here. Some things are handed to readers on a plate and others require further contemplation (which is encouraged, here). An openness to channeled spiritual messages is a prerequisite to appreciating these insights.

"*Humanity 2.0* is both a journal of discovery and a blueprint for reader change. It offers the unusual opportunity to draw together disparate threads of science, self-inspection and spiritual understanding and it covers both Earth change transitions now taking place and the process of individual and species transformation. Humans have many innate, unused abilities, and there are many methods of drawing them out. *Humanity 2.0* is one such resource, recommended for any new age reader open to a multitude of spiritual insights."

Bud Gardner, co-author *Chicken Soup for the Writer's Soul:* "This uplifting, inspirational, heartfelt book offers a unique plan for transforming one's life."

Writer's Digest contest judge: "In a time of bleak news dominating even bleaker TV news programs, death and wars on other continents, unrest here in the U.S. and abroad, and all the other ills of humanity, this is a rather amazing, uplifting and soulful little book on the hopefulness of the future. It's also a refreshing look at the New Humanity, our destiny as a nation and world community, our personal destiny, and the development of our Self...."

John S. Brennan, Founding Dean, Regis University's School for Professional Studies, Denver: "Of all the spiritual authors and texts I have read, *The New Humanity* is the most comforting, readable, and flowing. As a reader of over 95 books on spirituality and a career of 40+ years (teaching in adult learning psychology and mentoring 150 graduate folks through masters programs, both genders, diverse cultural backgrounds).... I am impressed.... This book has a clarity of notions and perspectives and use of words that reach hearts and create motivation in others to embrace the generic nature of spiritual issues, while not creating fear of personal recrimination for considering their inner voice by attending to and/or honoring their spirit's beckoning.... I am pleased and actually honored.... Charol has much to offer all of us."

Sedona Journal of Emergence: New & Notable: "... prophetic reflections on humanity's next evolutionary step...."

John W. Parker, Dialogues with Emerging Spiritual Teachers: "... reflects a growing awareness that the planet is going through a huge shift in consciousness...."

Marty Segal, New Age Publishing Co., Miami: "A welcome addition to the universal journey of awakening. Nicely done!"

Judith Coates, co-author of *Jeshua, The Personal Christ:* "The message in *The New Humanity* is wonderfully in alignment with the information we have been receiving...."

Barbara Munson, Circles of Life Foundation, *A Reason for Optimism:* "*The New Humanity* is for those of us who can see that the world is slowly changing for the better but who don't know how to change with it. Singularly positive and hopeful, this book made me feel good about myself while helping me understand who I am. It also made clear what I personally can do to speed up this process of achieving a beautiful new civilization. This is one book I will pass along to my family and friends."

Ursula Joy, Reiki master: "*The New Humanity* is fantastic! I could hardly put it down. Charol has a marvelous way of saying the most profound statements in an easy, casual way. This book is needed. It is truly written with spiritual insight. Charol is speaking truthfully and straightforward in a way that anyone can relate to. The writing is clear, uncluttered, and well put."

Linda Schiller-Hanna, clairvoyant and lightworker: "Charol Messenger's voice is untainted with ego. Here is a crystal-clear, heart-driven message that will bring you peace. The need for this book is enormous. Timely, profound and wise, it is sure to be a classic, referred to again and again."

Humanity Is on the Brink of Change

We have crossed an evolutionary threshold.

Humanity 2.0 heralds the new paradigm and offers a unique perspective on the planetary civilization that is our destiny and how we are creating that new society individually.[1]

No matter how things seem, no matter how much the world's noise is like a rumble letting loose across the airwaves, no matter how much the cries and desperation of millions are like a throttling of all hope, humanity, we are in a new life, struggling to find a new sense of Purpose. This is a new awareness piercing the density of the compelling dissonance. This is a new life threading through the very breath of all the confounding voices.

This unexpected expansion of humanity is very much the infusion of a stronger heart-consciousness. The conflicts in the various nations are an awakening cry, the anguish of prying free from old selfish dispositions, the surrender of ideas that have battered humanity from the beginning.

In *this* hour, humanity, we are shattering the old feelings of disconnection. We are holding ourselves up to a standard of compassion and involvement.

This century and the next, we will be seeing tremendous strides in our capacity to be more. Although we live in a time of uncertainty, we are in a time of renewal.

---

1 All further explored in *Wings of Light*, *The Soul Path*, and *The New Humans: Second Genesis*.

In a deep meditation, my oversoul spoke into my heart-mind and said, "My name is Samuel."

I saw him in a dream one quiet afternoon in Colorado during a short nap.

I looked up and this very handsome man in his forties walked toward me, dressed in a modest, brown monk's robe with a hood.

He came to me like a father. He came to me as a friend. He came without grandeur, but with a clear and steady gentleness.

And I knew: This is one called Oversoul. This one is the source of my being. This one is the purpose of my life, and I am to teach his message, given to each of us on Earth:

> "Be who you are, now, today. And fear not. For the true divinity, the wisdom, the strength, the guidance, is not an outer force or magic—but is you yourself.

> "*You* are the one who creates your life, your reality, your joy, your sorrow. *You* are the one with the power to change it.

> "The Divine Light is in all, without exception. You find that light when you pause in your busy life—and allow the breath of life to carry you into the womb of creation ... where you were born and always will exist.

> "You and all around you are a part of one Living Consciousness. And it is good. And so are you."

The Author

Futurist and global visionary Charol Messenger activated into Higher Self consciousness during a spontaneous awakening to cosmic consciousness and oversoul merge in 1975.[2]

Her books have received thirteen awards, including First Place Winner *The New Humans* (Book 2 *"The New Humanity"* series) in the Soul-Bridge Book Awards of Europe 2017 in the category "Spiritual Awakening of Humanity," as well as Second Place International Book Excellence Award 2017 (sole Finalist) in Spirituality; plus three more Book Excellence Awards in 2016 include: First Place Winner *You 2.0* in Personal Growth, and Second Place Winner *Humanity 2.0* (Book 1 in *"The New Humanity"* series, fourth award) (sole Finalist) in Spirituality.

A *spiritual revealer* attuned to the undercurrent hum sweeping through humanity, Charol has helped over 65,000 individuals through her Higher Self books, blogs, classes, tweets and 20,500 spiritual soul readings as a Higher Self clairvoyant.

A certified lightworker (1990), certified clear channel of Ascended Masters and the Spiritual Hierarchy (1983), and messenger of her oversoul and Angels of Serendipity, in the Messenger books Charol is revealing Higher teachings on spiritual development, the new millennial spirituality, Higher Self integration for everyday life, understanding the inner voice, communicating with the angels, and humanity's spiritual transcendence and long-foretold evolutionary transformation—that is happening *right now*. Humanity is in *transcension*. We are in it, now.

Founder of the Books for Iraq charity and international newsletter *Global Citizen*, Charol has a B.A. in English, philosophy, and world religions from the University of Colorado. She lives in Colorado with her Yorkshire Terrier.

---

2 For more on the oversoul, read *The Education of Oversoul Seven* by Jane Roberts, also my appendix "A Vision."

Also by Charol Messenger

THE NEW HUMANS (Series Book 2 "*The New Humanity*") – 2018 Second Edition. First Place Winner in Soul Bridge Book Awards of Europe 2017 in "Spiritual Awakening of Humanity." Second Place International Book Excellence Award (sole Finalist) in Body-Mind-Spirit.

HUMANITY 2.0 (Series Book 1 "*The New Humanity*") – 2018 Second Edition. Second Place Winner International Book Excellence Awards 2016 (sole Finalist) in Spirituality. National Finalist 2012 in *both* USA Best Books for New Age Nonfiction and CIPA EVVY in Spirituality. Third Place CIPA EVVY 2002 in Spirituality for the 1st Edition *The New Humanity* (replaced discontinued 2000 Xlibris edition) and is Vol. I in *Humanity 2.0* (all editions).

INTUITION FOR EVERY DAY (Series Book 3 "living your Higher Self") – 2018 Second Edition. Master Workbook on Enhancing Intuition. Meditations and techniques for: beginners, intermediate, and advanced. National Finalist USA Best Books 2015 in New Age Nonfiction.

YOU 2.0 (Series Book 2 "living your Higher Self") – 2018 Second Edition. Master Workbook on Higher Self initiation and integration. First Place Winner in International Book Excellence Awards 2016 in Personal Growth.

THE SOUL PATH (Series Book 1 "living your Higher Self") – 2018 Third Edition. Master Workbook on Becoming Fully Conscious. National Finalist USA Best Books 2015 in General Spirituality.

WINGS OF LIGHT (Series Book 1 "Angels") – 2018 Second Edition. Master Workbook on Connecting with the Four Angels Who Guide You. National Finalist CIPA EVVY 2012 in Spirituality.

WALKING WITH ANGELS (Series Book 2 "Angels") – 2018 Second Edition (in development, expanding, plus in print) (1st Ed. ebook retired).

I'M DANCING AS FAST AS I CAN (Series Book 1 Memoirs) – National Finalist USA Best Books 2005, memoir, vignette poetry.

All of the Messenger books include discussions of humanity's origin stories and evolution and our changing global society.

Contents

Volume I
The Prelude

Part I: What We and the World Will Be Like

The civilization that is humanity's destiny and the kind of people we will be.

Part II: How We Will Achieve the New Society

How we individually can become a new human and contribute to creating the new society.

Part III: Humanity's Heritage and Destiny

The origin of the human species, and our splendid destiny.

Volume II
Transcending

Part I: Humanity in Transformation

Part II: You the Bringer of Light

Appendices

Earth Change Transitions Now Taking Place

Symptoms of a Changing Earth

New Energy Source

Leashing the Forces of Nature

How to Remain Safe

My eternal love for my mom DJ who always believed in me. I dedicate all of these books to her, gentle and sweet spirit.

Also my love to my sister Jo, for our friendship.

My eternal gratitude to my dearest friend Barbara Munson for her irreplaceable support and friendship. She keeps me motivated and encouraged, and she is always there for me when I need another pair of eyes on final details.

My deep gratitude to Keith Klein and Mary Ann Klein. Their limitless grace allows me to do this fulfilling work with contentment.

My great appreciation to the thousands who have participated in the teachings given in these books; especially the *many* good souls who have gifted me throughout my life in innumerable ways, including: John Brennan, Marja Pheasant, JoAnn Goldsmith, Matthew Patterson, John Cloonan, and Ray Alcott.

Especially, I owe everything to the divine beings who guide me: my oversoul and soul council, the Angels of Serendipity, and the All Mind from whom all wisdom flows.

HUMANITY 2.0

Book 1 *"The New Humanity"* Series
on the Spiritual Awakening of Humanity

Second Edition
The New Humanity

Charol Messenger

The Awakening

The Divine Presence exuded through every cell of my being, nurturing every thought, attitude, and emotion. I had come out of a long inner darkness and a month of unexpected awakened intuitive abilities.

It was Sunday, November 2, 1975, two a.m. I was thirty years old, divorced, and living alone in my apartment in Colorado Springs, Colorado.

In the middle of this long dark night, a spontaneous mystical activation into cosmic consciousness shattered my self-image and transformed my sense of self, as if I had been picked up and set in the opposite direction.

My outpouring heart opened me to all the wisdom of the ages streaming into my consciousness. I poured myself wholly into the fullness of this new divine and ecstatic place of human beingness, and a tremendous euphoria filled me. I felt the grandeur of the Universal Consciousness—of which I then *knew* I was an integral part. For the first time, I had a sense of identity and a sense of purpose.

An irrepressible explosion of insight and wisdom whirled through me, transforming my small sense of self into something profound and larger. The world was suddenly filled with vibrant sounds, textures, images, and colors. Extra-ordinary grace expanded my imagination, hopes and desires, surpassing anything I had ever thought possible for my life. For the first time, I truly was stepping into, onto the edge of my future, my destiny.

Doubt succumbed to hope, possibility, potential, and all the extraordinary dreams that would keep me stretching. The shackles and blinders of my previous existence fell away and I saw my true life, the true world, and the true destiny of humanity and of each soul.

I saw the lights of every soul on earth. I saw us all transcending our small narrow lives, lifting up into our true light, our true nature. I saw who we really are: We are large. We are a grand species. We are individuals filled with the ideal Self.

It was in this revelatory moment, the culmination of many days of out-of-body visions and transcendent travels, that I knew why I was in this life, this world, this body.

The very next breath I took was the first breath of my new life. I breathed for the first time with the fullness of Spirit, with the heart of a gentle and valiant soul, with the mind of a seer and a teacher of wisdom, to remind us all who we really are. For we have always been this grand Self. None of us has ever stopped being this grand Self.

In this moment of my first breath, I saw the wholeness of us all. I saw our glad hearts. I saw and felt the smiles and laughter of our true Nature. I felt the yearning of our hearts for release from pain and anguish. I felt the cries of our true beings for peace and sanity. I felt the pull of all souls in the world to find a way to be reminded of their inner light, to find a way to rekindle that connection, to find a way to remember and once again live from that place of our deep Self that is sacred and free of all regret.

In that moment, Spirit set itself upon me. Spirit opened my heart, my mind, my eyes, my ears, my tongue; giving me gifts of knowing, knowledge of the inner worlds, knowledge of our true Selves, knowledge and understanding of what we are and what we once again can be, knowledge of where we are evolving as a people, knowledge of how to help individuals remember.

In this hour of awakening to my true Self, my destiny came upon me as a cloak of surrender, no matter what the cost; a cloak of sanctity to give all that I am to help the people of this world find even a moment or a glimpse of what I *knew* in this single hour.

Since that day, I have had many hours, at times many months, of uninterrupted bliss and a continuous glow in the rapture of the Divine Presence breathing its force through me, that I may fulfill my purpose—which is to rekindle the *memory* of what we all are: divine beings.

That tremendous surging Vital Force still pushes me to transcend my everyday reality and to continue to reach out—because that is how we grow, that is how we each have made it this far, how we have always evolved and become more as a people and as individuals.

Awakened to my divine Nature, the fullness of Spirit flooded my being, flushed, purged, and nurtured my every thought and feeling to be a voice of the Divine, a hand of the Divine, to share with others whatever the Divine gives through me.

Graced by the splendid touch of God, thereafter transformed, I gave over my life wholly to be of service. That was the beginning of my life and the opening of my journey into my heart.

We are the Divine. We are all precious. Every single one of us is a spark of the *Divine All Knowing Presence* we call God. God speaks through us every day—through our lives. That is what God is. God is *us* when we are being our wholeness.

Introduction

Volume I is the main body of *Humanity 2.0,* received through the Universal Consciousness during a period of exceptionally heightened awareness in 1994. This volume was initially published in 2000 as *The New Humanity,* again in 2001 with a better cover. In 2012, I incorporated it into *Humanity 2.0,* first edition, prior to the December 21 Mayan prophecy, to offset people's worries about the end of times—because I *knew* from all the writings I had been receiving that the humans species is only just beginning.

Volume II is essays on individual and societal transformation, which we are now undergoing.

Appendices include university thesis papers, "Being Within the Oneness" and "Holism: A New Trend in Humanity's Consciousness" on Mind-Body Interaction, Elements of a Whole Self: A definition of soul.

Volume I

The Prelude

Part I

What We and the World Will Be Like

*The civilization that is humanity's destiny
and the kind of people we will be.*

1

On the Brink of a New Society

We are changing our perceptions about reality and altering the way we view life. We are learning to release our fears and inhibitions and to allow healing and expansive attitudes, to invite change and even embrace it.

The era we are now entering has every possibility of being the most extraordinary since the beginning of human existence. We are in a transition from the overbearing premise of, "Only help another if it will help yourself."

In a time not far distant—an era of increased compassion—humanity will access the higher wisdoms instantly. Already we are beginning to change emotionally and physically in our personalities and bodies. We are in transition spiritually and mentally. These may not be noticeable at times, because until now we have confused values with social standards and ethics with what is legal, and we have not been in sync with the cosmic whole that can direct our every thought.

How do we open our inner awareness and access spiritual understanding and reasoning in order to eliminate fear and frustration and illuminate the path of life before us? How do we unleash the complete Presence that is within us? How are we able to be unflinching in the face of disaster? The Divine Mind teaches:

Honor yourself.

Evaluate your inner struggles and beliefs that may have narrowed your experiences of joy.

Strive to understand the forces that rule human nature.

Give of your heart—in an attuned way—to others who struggle to understand the seeming loss of control over their lives.

Humanity's innate inner knowledge of how all of us are connected gives us the capacity to shift focus from the one to the whole; as well as the ability to envision and link compassionately with every other person and life form, including animals.

Society's wounds are but extensions of our individual wounds of the heart and soul. We are able to heal these wounds. We are able to reconstruct our personalities and to function as enlightened and balanced persons.

Every person is innately imbued with divine inspiration and inner knowing. Every person has access to the inner resonance ... that *still small inner voice* that prompts and counsels us from within.

When not attuned to our spiritual Nature, the inner voice seems in conflict with our own desires and against what we accept as reality. However, the inner voice is the most illumined aspect of our being. The inner voice is the consciousness we name God.

Without the inner voice to guide us, we do not live as our true Self, because the human personality is bound to repeated routine. The inner voice teaches us to imagine, envision, and expand our understanding of what is possible. The inner voice brings us certainty in every circumstance.

With this concept tangible in our lives, we connect to our spiritual power, our conscience is open and clear, and we develop inner reasoning and align with our true Self.

Through *Mind*—which is *all* of us—we understand the workings of spiritual law and we realize the strategic plan of the Universal Stream of Consciousness. When we attach our desires to spiritual concepts, we are guided into realms that surpass known laws of nature.

When we live from our inner light, we are not afraid of any person or situation. We know what is truth and what is not. We change how we experience ourselves and how we relate to others. Our ideas expand. Our mind becomes limitless. Our emotions heal. Our body changes. Our spirit fills with a love for all.

These are the elements of the new society we are all creating and becoming. Humanity is transcending its old patterns of behavior. We are evolving new attitudes and new social actions—one person at a time.

Every person who is rising into the Divine Mind and releasing personality to Divine Will is becoming a new human. A new human is kind and tolerant, knows inner strength, and experiences life as an exciting adventure where every unexpected turn is a mystery to be explored.

This state of being is unfolding now in all of humanity, one person at a time. Once the whole of us reaches the concept of the all rather than the one, the fabric of human society will shift to a new level of human existence.

2

The World As It Will Be

Humanity is embarking upon a fortunate time. We are realigning our perceptions and attitudes and less often seeing the unpleasant aspects of life as catastrophic. We are learning new and honorable behaviors. We are reforming mentally, realizing that what we concentrate on is what we create, and that what we attend to mentally and emotionally is the reality we steep ourselves within.

As a whole, humanity will reach a saturation point with anger. We will be filled with a distaste for ugliness and we will no longer tolerate anguish. We will treat the odd characteristics of society with remorse and no longer fuel distemper. We will abolish views of titillation over the absurd and improbable.

Once all of humanity are receptive to cooperation and alignment with the highest good of all, we will have constructed a new society: thinkers who admire goodwill and discernment.

Our lives depend on how clearly we define honesty, hope, and peace-loving behaviors. We require devotion to and conscious awareness of every person's reasons, motivations, and anticipations. Once we apply intuitive insight to all of our decisions and actions, that is the society we will create.

Physical laws are a byproduct of our mental and emotional consciousnesses. Consequently, physical manifestation can be directed mentally, even focused willfully and with intentioned results.

Humanity actually will acquire procedures to link with every other person whom we previously found disturbing. This form of reanalyzing what substantially is important to humanity's continued existence will become a central issue in society. We will be so enamored with goodwill and the balance of opinions that we will disengage ourselves from extreme examples of denial and powerlessness. We will reframe our viewpoints to being active consciously in the wellness process.

Once we realize that we can live in harmony with people who are unlike us, we will change our understanding about the purpose of being human. We will acquire such a scope of wisdom that we will initiate procedures that foster hope, power, and reason. We will keep our thoughts to ourselves, display no arrogance or hostility, reason before acting, amuse ourselves with kindness, live in humor, forgive all errors, live calmly and with tolerance, and reframe our own point of view to the whole.

These procedures will guide us into becoming more socially aware. We will learn to reason in balance with other people's needs and desires and not to contemplate only our own willful nature. The possibility of compromise will begin to root in us. We will be sensitive to the positions of others, and we will care what happens to them. In the new society, it will be abnormal to be uncaring.

Humanity's innate Nature is to live at-one with all. In fact, that is how the human species will survive. Reanalyzing our attitudes will become imperative as the earth reconstructs, because survival will depend upon each one of us being fully able to reach a state of harmony. Embracing cooperation is how we will enhance our lives.

When we are attuned to the whole of life, we have learned an essential lesson: to reassess our values and to accept newer behaviors—honor and cooperation.

When we are renewed by our spiritually centered Identity, we view life with eagerness rather than fear what might come. We view life as remarkable rather than as placidly boring with monotonous day-to-day redundancy. When our heart is awakened, serenity infuses us and alters our experiences in life.

In the new society, we will forgive our unknowing nature and reposition our beliefs toward reason. Our senses will fill with hope, because we will touch our innate potentiality given to us when we were created by the All That Is. This potentiality will be the crux of the new society.

In the times to come, traits normal in our daily routine will be finer insight, reasoning by love, being humble in the face of Providence's power, and accepting responsibility to embark upon a more holy avenue of personal expression.

We will grasp higher reason, focus on grand proportions, and imagine any possible solution to any problem. We will no longer subject others to ridicule. Rather, we will fulfill our own inner Nature by listening to our inner being.

Our imagination will unfold in full array, and we will bestow blessings upon all people by our kind temperament. We will assess circumstances that fill our heart, and we will direct our actions favorably and without desperation. We will dwell in a serene mind and spirit and contemplate our individual uniqueness. We will visualize the greater spectrum of how our talents may be useful to the whole. We will appreciate our innate sweetness and bring it forth as the nectar of our true disposition.

Sweetness is inherent in us. Sweetness is a fragrance born from spiritual insight. When nurtured, sweetness permeates and vitalizes our lives. When we embrace our sweetness, it becomes the mode by which we exist.

When we dwell on caution, we live in fear; when we dwell on confidence, we live in the clarity of the inner counselor. When we dwell on beliefs of separation and futility, we live in anger and frustration and our choices are abusive and misguided; when we dwell on anger, we live in anger. When we dwell on trust, we create hope and delight; when we dwell on harmony, we create equality and fairness, and society is blessed by our demeanor. As we overcome our dissonant traits, we reach toward others in kindness.

In the times to come, the criteria by which humanity will be measured is how we relate to each other. Attuned visionary behavior and illumined thinking will be the norm. We will be so devoted to wellness—mentally, physically, and emotionally—that we will be unable to conceptualize any other approach toward people's illnesses and misguided actions. We will perceive them and their circumstances with clarity and understanding.

This does not mean we will tolerate antisocial or dangerous behaviors. We will do what we can to help those people, but we will not encourage their integration into society until they are well. In the new society, we will nurture the whole, because it is the whole that we all are.

When a single cell is anti-constructive, it is a danger not only to others but to itself. In the times ahead, we will tolerate no dissonant behaviors. Persons with a vindictive character will be considered a danger to society. Those who learn to perceive becoming a blessing to others will exhibit a change of heart and a change of attitude.

Humanity will recognize that the inner counselor is a personal guide. In the times ahead, we will listen to our inner being and focus within to foster wellness, in ourselves as well as others, such as those who grow up angry and afraid.

Each of us is seeded with goodness and higher perception. When we are not afraid of life's mysteries, and we grasp life's challenges with full interest, we acquire inner peace, which establishes the fine beings we innately are.

Tapping the anguish of our lives is like puncturing an infected sore. Once the discoloration of our spiritual Nature runs clear, our sweetness (as if an angel's touch upon us) exudes from our inner being and heals us like a medication of the gods.

Sweetness is a primary instinctual behavior that can saturate us until it becomes our entire perspective on life. The world as it will be is what we are becoming today.

3

The World As We Know It Ending

We are always adjusting to living by our higher Nature. We are always rekindling how to believe in ourselves and to see ourselves as intelligent and loving. Once we discover our spiritual Self, we are filled with hope, patience, and trust in our capacity to rise above our limitations and failures.

Life is not smooth and unobstructed. Once we distinguish the natural difficulties of life from what we believe is the way life should be, we no longer misconstrue what life is or suffer from blind perceptions.

The world is on the brink of change. What matters most is that we individually are changing.

As we become accustomed to our inner spiritual power, we no longer feel lost within society. We are better able to resist the temptations that daily bombard us, and we better focus our lives through the insights of our spiritual Nature.

Nothing that happens is a final force that shapes our personality. We choose what will affect our mood. We use higher reason, which enables us to let go of hatred, anger, judgment, and fear. We learn to forgive and to see all peoples and circumstances as whole, rather than only by their effect on our personal life.

The human personality responds to our life events according to how we see ourselves. As we become alive with hope and perceive our ideal Nature, we infuse ourselves with compassion for the disillusionment that belittles our self-esteem. We see how our life might result from our insights and actions, by rekindling the definitive presence of our *inner knowing self* and realizing that the world does not cause who we are.

Daily and ongoing self-initiated karma is the universal natural law of cause and effect, which is a component of all life. When we restyle our attitudes, we are restyling the direction toward which we are evolving both spiritually and in our manifest physical life. When we support other people's dreams and desires, the more our own conscience instructs us on how to better serve the whole of humanity. The more we strive to live from our true capacity, the more we rise into social consciousness as a standard by which to live.

Society does not delineate our individual character. Rather, each of us delineates the evolution of humanity. What each of us perceives, understands, and applies becomes a part of the character of the whole. The more individuals who believe in living by spiritual compassion and insight—rather than living on the edge according to the perceived status quo—the more this will become the view of all society.

Every person is significantly affecting the nature of life, because everything each of us is extends into what humanity becomes. In time, the world will reshape according to our fondest common hopes and dreams.

The evolution of humanity is a composite process. The species will survive and evolve, because the greater number of us are filling ourselves with a belief in higher truth. We are not defining what that truth must be nor what that truth must look like. We are merely accepting that higher knowledge is a way to learn to live more humanely and with greater satisfaction and fulfillment.

The world is changing because each of us is changing. What we are is altering. Our attitudes are fluid and in flux. Our beliefs are moving toward the clarity of the precious inner power.

Everything we imagine is possible, both good and bad. Therefore, to create a good society, it is essential to believe in humanity's innate goodness.

Hope is an important commodity. Hope is the sunlight of our souls. It is a fragrance of divine vision.

As we invest in our higher sensitivity, hope predominates in our personality as a guiding principle for all of our beliefs and desires. We change our attitudes to comprehend more easily the fluctuating beliefs and standards of what is right by believing in our self-worth. We draw conclusions by analyzing other people's strategies and behaviors. We assume that other people can establish their own workable solutions. We establish our own in order to acquire the precious insight.

To discover the fears that may obscure your own perspective:

- Create a view of life that is aligned with your heart.

- *Thoughtfully* apprise others of your personal opinions about the actions of society.

- Assess what matters and what does not.

- If ever you fear the consequences of your decisions, re-evaluate what is important in your own life.

- Create the attitude of living at-one with all persons.

When we are able to assess our own actions as honorable and nondestructive, we are able to create and foster hope. That is how we manifest the precious inner power.

To be free from dismay:

- Deliver yourself from self-denial.

- Reacquaint yourself with your innate better Nature.

- Surround yourself with the higher wisdom from the Unseen Protectors of higher thought.

- Assume a new impression of how to attest to the new vision that humanity is transcending its patterns of thought, and someday the old ways of life will no longer be important to you.

To reassess your actions and enable yourself to comprehend your inner light, alter your insights. For example, with an affirmation such as:

"I am a loving person, and I believe in loving people."

When we observe that humanity is despairingly overwrought by difficulties and challenges, we begin to dissipate within ourselves— for all time—the false belief that humanity's inherent tendencies of unspeakable destruction are truisms of our own individual nature.

We then reassess our hopes and dreams and their viability as a depiction of humankind's potential, because whatever we personally experience, humanity will experience eventually. Whatever we personally aspire to as ideal, humanity will aspire to eventually, because each of us is a single cell within the whole.

When we are shaping our new Self, our insights direct the movement of the consciousness of the whole and our considerable individual leverage affects the order of society toward a higher sensitivity and awareness.

This is so because when we accept ourselves as instrumental to reality, we begin re-establishing the universal powers as a shaping force in our lives. With a view of respect, we understand that society is redesigning based upon mutuality in everyone's point of view.

As we restyle the way we think and behave, we accept that every person is a part of all humanity and is a living consciousness extended both from and to the whole. This vision defines our personal experiences as a member of the social stream.

Shifting perception becomes not something that happens to us without our knowledge or awareness, but results from our individual conceptualizing of what can be and our personal effort toward being more compassionate and amused about the less desirable experiences of this world. We are then better able to manage our emotions and better align our passions.

Humanity is beginning to formulate this kind of world. The new society is becoming realized fundamentally. All that we perceive as truth is to some degree subject to change, depending upon what we perceive truth to be.

When our mind is open to envisioning that truth is subjective, for the most part we realize that all of our experiences in life are subjective. This realization expands our ability to comprehend, integrate, allow, enjoy and forgive; because we then have increased our capacity to see others as precious and integral to the whole of life. We realize that every person is necessary, because each of us contributes through our own process.

Together, through our unique desires, wills, and actions born from self-esteem, we are recreating society. Through our visions, anticipation and certainty, we are reshaping the world. Our individual and joint lives reflect the consciousness of humanity.

Integrated as a truth, this is the foundation of the new strategy upon which all of humanity soon will begin to live.

4

The Present As It Is Completing

Let us evaluate our lives as they are today. What are we defusing emotionally? What are we reconstructing?

We have been instituted socially to believe in our "voidness," which has made it difficult to discover our higher Nature. Yet as we improve in optimism, humanity is undergoing a change in point of view about what is healthy in our actions toward others.

Everything to which we devote ourselves—helping others, feeding others, teaching others—is like feeding a garden at the root level. We are watching humanity grow step by step. This is the process of the human race becoming stronger and wiser.

Wisdom is innate in the human spirit. Every person can access the higher wisdom. Every person can be alive with the spirit of the Divine. When we align with our personal purpose in life, what we attend to carefully, consistently, and continuously will result eventually in the very fulfillment that we seek.

To believe that what you envision is good for you and you are worthy of it, instill yourself with those very private contemplations about your own place in the world. Nurture at the root level the seedling of your cosmic being.

Our continuous devotion to our vibrant and living spiritual Nature—nurturing a *new* reason for our life to continue—enables us with hope. Know that your desires and dreams *will* come to pass and that what you know in your inner Self will ring true for others; because your inner experiences, although personal, are simultaneously cosmic.

We are all learning to accept our spiritual power. We are learning that we are connected to The Good, and we are learning to embrace the qualities that constitute a good nature.

Every person is essential to the fabric of life. Each person's perceptions are integral to the evolution of humanity into a more fantastic existence than we have ever known.

All that humanity has imagined is now coming to pass. What we have hoped for is birthing. The goodness we have stored and built upon is now taking hold. These centuries have not been a waste of time. The constancy of humanity's common vision is leading us into the realm we have imagined and hoped for.

You can recognize this by listening with your heart, your *inner knowing self,* which makes right choices aligned with the Divine for your own benefit and the benefit of all.

Our heart guides us clearly and in truth. Our individual perspectives and actions are integral to the whole expression that unfolds in humanity. When we perceive something enthusiastically within the very essence of our being, there is nothing of which we are incapable, nothing we are unable to do.

The purpose of human life is to learn our true place in the whole. People want to trust and live in peace. As we reach our zenith of purposeful self-awareness and we feel the summit of our coping skills, we achieve a synchronicity between our physical personality and the delighted Universe. Our most remarkable achievements are consequences of the extraordinary contentment that arises from alignment with the inner resonance.

When attuned to our higher Nature, we assess our actions in a way that is free of judgment, ridicule, and condemnation. We are no longer perplexed about needing to be perfect. We mature intentionally and with a spiritual reasoning capacity. We understand what will develop our innate kind Nature. We feel our inner spiritual Nature motivating and strengthening us. We resonate in exquisite harmony with all of life.

Humanity can change and grow. Our ability to comprehend circumstances beyond our current experience is fashioning us into an extraordinary people. All that we have learned to incorporate in our personal awareness is altering the world.

It is time to assess our human dramas compassionately. As we each come to value our own personality, we can then comprehend our personal strengths and potential contribution to the human drama.

5

Our Lives As They Are Transcending

By developing an honorable temperament, we rise into our admirable true Nature and a life that is amazing and delightfully expanding.

Imagine that humanity has risen from its distemper, that we understand how to be socially successful, and that we are devoted to being at-one with each other.

In the world of tomorrow, we will frequent inner joy more than outer stimulation. We will frequent inspired understanding of various disciplines of self-awareness more than the intoxication of delusions, which we will realize are based on fear. We will alleviate our catastrophic pains from excruciating self-judgment by awakening the inner healer. We will devise a respite from the horrible angers that have suffocated our light. We will alleviate the distresses that have suffocated our preciousness. By believing in our oneness, we will alleviate our uncertainty in all of our pursuits.

When we attend to our spiritual Self's grievances, we discover a safe yet healing self-analysis of our most secret fears. We reassess what we care about and what we define as necessary for evolving into our spiritual Nature.

In the times ahead, humanity's behaviors will focus toward self-generating compassion and forgiveness. We will lean on the real distinction between higher actions and ordinary reasoning. We will transcend self-destruction in favor of our wiser Nature. We will believe in the Life Presence as a guiding force for our decisions. We will focus our efforts more humbly. We will no longer be overwhelmed by premises of self-preservation. Rather, we will concentrate on accessing our godself.

Once humanity has begun integrating this process, we will institute a form of free-thinking that will inspire and uplift us. Self-analysis will be less divisive. We will be more aware of how to enhance our greater Character. We will endow ourselves and each other with hope and a belief in esoteric realities. We will no longer restrict our precious Identities to fathomless falsehoods about reality. Rather, we will enjoy unlimited possibilities of perception, which range from the "I" to the whole.

We will bridge the disenchantment that has been our suffering to believing in honor as the intelligent path, which also is the means by which humanity will survive. We will consider how we are all more alike than different. We will enjoy the friendships of many rather than the smothering attachments of a few. We will no longer judge others as false, but we will see every person with humor and patience. We will no longer live based on separation but will comprehend the singular origin and singular destiny of all humanity.

This change in focus will not take place in a single hour or a single day, but over many decades, many. Nevertheless, the ultimate result of the path humanity is now treading is an assured *group consciousness.*

In place of despair, we will nurture confidence. In place of uncertainty, we will nurture fairness. We will lean upon the attributes of being *soul-infused.*

This attitude will alter the way we perceive ourselves, until we live instinctually as if no other person is our enemy. We will cooperate, or agonize from the lack of it (until we learn to let go and let be).

As humanity embraces spiritual perceptions, we will embrace our new Identities. We will completely reassess ourselves and believe in our innate extrasensory Nature. We will invoke cosmic awareness as a precious commodity upon which all else depends for our success as spiritual human beings.

We will reconsider what is unacceptable behavior, no longer needing to fear being judged or criticized. Such actions will be uncommon and we will find them difficult to imagine. We will no longer be overcome by ineptness. Rather, we will know our spiritual power and incorporate it in everything we do.

Our lives will then unfold as if by magic. Yet it is natural, because the unfolding is a consequence of healing our attitudes toward ourselves and others.

We will so alter our intentions and willfulness that we will no longer fumigate ourselves with ridicule or self-denial. We will comprehend our sensitive spiritual consciousness and be absorbed with developing it.

Humanity, we are a part of each other. Each of us is a single cell within the Cosmic Consciousness we name God. Each of us is a thread within the universal fabric of life. Humanity's survival and existence depends upon us individually grasping the unitary framework of all life forces. Each of us, whom we think of as a separate self, is a reflection of a central *Nature*. Together, we comprise a single unit of *Thought Expression*.

In the midst of our strifes and wars, we will begin to see the erroneous and futile misnomers of our previous false perceptions. We will release our concerns over our differences. We will see how each person and living being is an aspect of a whole consciousness.

The new society will reflect our innate spiritual Selves. By exploring our unique Character, we will see that we are all alike, merely individually studying facets of this incredible experience we call life.

Part II

How We Will Achieve the New Society

*How we individually can become a new human
and contribute to creating the new society.*

6

Becoming a New Human

Opening our awareness toward hope is the most important thing we can do toward becoming a new human. How do you do this?

- See yourself gently.

- Grasp the truth of yourself—that you are a magnificent spiritual being.

- Live fully with a conscious mind, tranquil heart, and invigorated physical body.

To transcend personality traits that may demoralize you or destroy unity, live consciously with an intention of goodwill, actions of fairmindedness, and beliefs in honor.

To know your bright reflection, totally immerse in your higher awareness (higher consciousness).

To achieve higher awareness:

- Alleviate the delusions that may currently define your life.

- No longer champion hatred or disillusionment.

- Rather, embrace the incredible goodness of your *inner knowing self.*

- Assume a focus and intention that surpass disenchantment.

- Reawaken the inner peace that is limitless, boundless, and continuous.

- Bridge the differences between you and others.

Forgiveness, tranquility, and a gentle nature are our innate Character. In those moments when we are free of confusion, we may be enlightened as to the purpose of our personal life and the purpose of humanity's existence, as well as ways to surpass paralyzing fears. Our personal reality depends upon our experiences of various options that come to our awareness.

To appreciate your remarkableness, live from the divine perceptions of your *inner knowing self.*

Humanity's true nature and dominant characteristic is a generosity of spirit. When we see this in ourselves, that is when we lift into that Identity and live for the good of all. When we actively engage this attribute with all the fervor and blessedness we can muster, that is when we lift into our finest hour and become a light in the world.

We lift into being a new human by living as a representative of all that is good by reflecting in all of our actions our spiritual Nature and by giving back to life an abundance of joy in everything we do.

The new humanity begins with each of us aware of our value and actively involved in the experience of being human. Humanity is an extension of our *combined* singleness of mind. The new humanity will be each of us fully realized.

7

Raising Our Vision of Ourselves

We are all *earthborn*. In the new society, this common perspective will raise our vision of ourselves.

To be unaffected by the conditions in the world, to uplift your own vision into a higher awareness, and to reach a calm and balanced spirit:

- Create order in your own life.

- Find strength through your inner Character.

- Achieve serendipity by striving to live as a spiritual master every day.

- Explore and use your imagination.

- Keep hope in your plans and promises.

- Enhance yourself through grand disciplines; such as, meditation, yoga, prayer.

- Live by new standards: *"Be kind ... Live humbly."*

- Restore happiness in yourself in every situation.

- Listen carefully to other people's ideas.

- Utilize other people's original thoughts in some way.

- Believe in the essential goodness of every person.

- Live each day fully self-aware and in harmony with all of life.

- Reassess false beliefs that bog down your visionary concepts.

- Reach toward life with an open mind toward all people and circumstances.

- Understand that consequences are a reflection of your beliefs and attitudes.

- Kindle faith in your capacity to rise above the dilemmas that plague you.

- Reach out for resourceful solutions. They may seem impossible, but the results will be substantial.

Our inner strength is greater than any dilemma. Sometimes it does not seem possible to live as our heart wants. Sometimes it is a great challenge and seems too much to grasp.

To uplevel your life:

- Become *still.*

- Live without abrasive interactions.

- Trust that all avenues are accessible when pursued in alignment with a higher cause.

- Believe that your personality is reconstructing and becoming more amenable.

- Believe that all animals have a kindred spirit to humanity.

- Understand that life is an expression of natural law.

- See every person as a part of a whole force.

- Rearrange your personal agenda if, in the moment, the highest definition of your being requires you to be elsewhere.

- Listen inwardly for the counsel of the angels.

- Reposition your attitudes to surrendering false pride.

- Imagine possibilities.

Saturating our actions and imagination with these criteria stimulates positive changes in our lives. Success is a process.

Historically, humans have not been cognizant of the values that are now paramount in our culture. It is as if our true Selves have been encased in concrete, as if we have been marble statues, facsimiles.

Humanity will become more spiritually aware than we are today. In the times ahead, we will be more introspective, visionary, and intelligent regarding solutions to the difficulties we face. We will better decipher and improvise how to resolve our struggles, because we will be enchanted with our spiritual Nature.

Humanity is approaching a level of living that will surpass known discoveries about styles of communication, complexity, and synchronicity. Human consciousness is stretching in such a way that it will become commonplace to devote ourselves to being reverent toward all. We will engage an extraordinary sense of self-appreciation, which will invoke a capacity to appreciate others. We will believe of others, *"You are glorious."* We will comprehend the range of affections that compose reality, and we will embody those affections in our traits and behaviors. We will feel the presence of the living God in the world around us, and we will no longer be afraid.

Becoming spiritually awake is not remarkable. It is a natural process toward which we are moving. We are being consumed with the fabric of love.

Everything we do and say is like a thread of cosmic awareness imprinting itself on our socialization—individually and as a whole. We are going forward. We are becoming purified of the notions that have burdened our common awareness. We are becoming able to live with a sense of devotion to all that is good. We are becoming one.

8

The Swift Alterations in Our Lifestyles

Our purpose for being physical is to assess our individual values, appreciate the common strengths that guide us, uncover the beauty in our being, and restore an affection for all of life.

When we accept our loving Nature, in all situations, we are no longer misguided by desire or greed, because we are at-one with our gentle Self.

To maintain equilibrium and energize your spiritual power, expand in awareness and approach higher consciousness as a form of your true Identity.

Humanity has forgotten that the whole of us shifts as a result of each person's experiences, that our personality defines our individual process and leads us into avenues previously unknown and untried so that we may grow.

When we lift into the higher vision of our *inner knowing self*, we are able to believe in the higher laws that guide us. When we do, we begin living as a natural being.

Walking the path of believing that the Life Forces guide, shelter, protect, and enhance us changes the way we view life. No matter what happens or what dangers possess us, we feel fortunate in our ability to live fairly—with humility and pride, grace and courage, sensitivity and power. These qualities amplify the inner wisdom and direct us so that we are able to reach new heights in this world that is ascending in consciousness.

Within a developing embryonic state of being, such as humanity is now experiencing, the effects of a single life force resonate and ripple throughout all other experiences and personalities.

Our chief personal responsibility is to live from our spiritual Nature, because living in personality means falling into disarray and chaos by way of emotions and judgments.

We find the inner power by devoting ourselves to living to the best of our ability every day. The inner power results from our earnest effort at living in balance with all. The *key* to maintaining equilibrium during catastrophic occurrences is compassion for ourselves and others. The *keys* to maintaining our spiritual being and spiritual life are compassion and the ability to reason from a higher perspective.

To comprehend catastrophic episodes:

- Look upon them from a point of view that is broader than your own personal needs and desires.

- Direct and focus your passions to their fullest potential, which extends your mind and presence.

- Live with a true concentration upon the passions that motivate you.

- Acquire concentration as a result of a continuous effort to resonate with all, as if your own voice is a single musical note within a great orchestra.

- Reassess continuously what kind of person you are, always improving and attuning to the vision of your inner Nature.

- Bring into your experience this vision of hope and purpose, which are the threads that hold you together in the midst of chaos.

These elements formulate the greatest and deepest mysteries, yet enable us to comprehend opportunities. By living these elements, we can live fully in a clear mind rather than be absorbed by confusion or undisciplined reactions.

Our personal destiny is in our own hands, not through effort but as a function or extension of our concentration. By directing our concentration with all of the splendor we feel moving through us when we pray, we can access the higher intelligence within us. By our greater conviction and closer knitting of the innate spiritual power, we can live as one with the life forces of nature and humanity.

We are living during an era of unparalleled growth of our personalities and spiritual Nature. Whether we are attuned to the world's infatuations or are more interested in being alive with spirit, the world is changing. Patterns of global and personal behaviors are shifting. Everything we are doing is reconstructing us into a frequency of compassion.

Within this enormous form of strengthening our spirits, we are grasping attitudes that will shape and fill the world with joy. Some of those attitudes are unfamiliar because we have not relied on our true Nature. Some of the attitudes synchronize with directing our concentration to being more attuned. Everything we conceptualize as necessary becomes a formula for our spiritual beings. As we become more compassionate, we learn that the reality in which we live, as an adult, is exactly what we have created it to be.

When we address our inner consciousness regularly and live within its vibration, we assess our needs and wishes from a different measure. We accept synchronicity as a way of life and differences as potential strengths, and we energize our body through a continuous application of integrity in all that we do. This is what heals us and will heal our world.

When we apply a fair portion of effort to our endeavors, we reap an abundance of serendipitous opportunities and circumstances and an abundance of feelings that are sweet and serene.

Potentially, human life is a vision of wonder. The new world we are shaping will extend from our personal beliefs and desires. The new world will reflect the people we are becoming.

To live harmoniously:

- Strategize fairly and with equal submission to goodness.

- Visualize harmony in every action and intention.

- Compose formulas of operation that will implement goodwill.

- Surrender self-worship as no longer a model for living.

- Communicate honorably.

- Live with a clear conscience, and be prepared to modify your behavior patterns if they mislead you.

- Simplify your fraternal obligations.

- Openly attend to all people and beings who cross your way, who need service, devotion, or affection.

These guidelines shield us from unnecessary pain and encourage us in directions and to programs for a whole and enhancing lifestyle that is unique and personal.

With such behaviors, we are able to rethink any posturing that does not support the whole and able to construct our own posturing to an equitable arrangement with others ... because what humanity is about is not rigidity. We are ever evolving, ever reconstructing in our behaviors and visions. We are ever delineating a more pure expression of the spirit burgeoning from within us.

To make your life sublime, hold a vision of yourself that is lovely, dynamic, and fair. Find a common ground of exchange that enhances your personality.

9

The New Values and
Ethical Guidelines

How do our personal judgments, idiosyncrasies, and discriminations influence the populace? What social influences shape our beliefs and values? How can we believe that each person is important and necessary to the well-being of everyone?

To help create an illumined society, we heal our own negative attitudes and awaken in ourselves new perceptions of what are right actions, right beliefs, and right values. We learn to perceive our innermost Self; we see how self-will, personal experiences, attitudes, and devotions direct our own life, and how we are integrally connected to every other person.

In the new society, we will be aware of our own influence on others in this psychological way just as today we are aware of the effect of the physical environment on our health. In fact, the psychological and physical are synchronous; each affects the other. What we "stew" about mentally sets a tone and energy pattern in the world around us.

This expanding vibration, like a stone thrown into a pond, generates pathological reasoning and behaviors that result in antipathy, apathy, judgment, sarcasm, and willfulness, at the expense of everyone. If we ourselves expend such an energy, we are not shielded from its effects, either; in fact, we are the most affected.

More than that, we are imbuing our own personal pattern of self-deception upon all of humanity, because *we* are a part of the world and everything anyone does influences everyone else.

The human personality requires attunements just as an automobile requires tune-ups. Our body and psyche are vehicles of our spiritual consciousness. Following are attitudes that cause us to be less than we are:

We credit ourselves with imagination yet dilute our potency by muddying our aspirations by being bitter, critical, or disagreeable. We pollute the social strata with unkept promises and bemoanings of lost dreams. We weaken our spiritual strength and guidance by ridiculing others. We live with conflicting decisions and do not anticipate harmony; rather, we succumb to disharmony as natural, and we regard failure as natural. We perceive recklessness as exciting and see it as imposing a godlike power. We subjugate insight and intuition as meaningless drivel. We compromise sensitivity, calling it stupidity. We complain repeatedly and dramatically.

We of humanity are about to straighten out in our lives a composition of vital viewpoints and realizations. We may be unused to serendipity as a way of life, yet such grace truly can be our reality. We can learn to exhibit a state of mind and emotions that revere life and honor others, because when we feel worthy we see worth in others.

To attune to your spiritual being and grasp the vital traces of your potent Self, affirm:

I am an aspect of the Divine Mind and Divine Will, a living expression of the whole of life.

Everything I do matters, for me and for others.

I live every day instilled with the vital presence of Mind, to be an asset to the world around me.

I vitalize my uniqueness and awaken creativity within me; from which come instinct, insight, intuition, and knowing.

I choose, will, and behave in accordance with the laws of the universe and the goodwill of all.

All people suffer, as we ourselves suffer. To live as an enlightened person, be thoughtful and conscientious in all avenues of experience.

To change the way you exist, choose to live by values that enhance everyone.

To acquire trust, be devoted to the higher presence of Mind. Explore your personal presence as an example of the Creative Power. Assume a higher framework of action and sensitivity. Applaud your mistakes as ingredients to nurture further trust of the higher powers.

If engulfed by errors, turn your attention to your higher consciousness, within which you may analyze situations and attain wisdom and guidelines to help you change your circumstances.

If things go wrong, turn to the wisdom *within* for direction and to access perceptions that can lead you to new directions and opportunities that, before, you could not even imagine.

Historically, we humans have feared what we do not understand. A wise person seeks understanding of the unusual and unfamiliar. By investing ourselves with the processes of *inner linking* with the Causative Consciousness, we can realize how valuable we are and how valuable each person is.

Even if we feel inconsequential compared to the Universal Presence, when we absorb that Presence into our focus of being, we stretch into realms of thought and belief that previously may have been beyond our capacity to comprehend. This discovery fills us with such hope that we live truly in devotion to our higher reasoning Self.

We learn, thereby, to structure our existence based on living the ideals of the spiritual world. When we do, we find that life extraordinarily transforms into a passionate reflection of our greatest dreams.

During the struggles and challenges of life, when we walk the pathway of higher sensitivity, we glimpse, then embrace, a perception something like:

Anything I am, I can change today.

Anything I have been, I can alter in this moment.

What I wish to be, I can be ... through my dedication and my thoughts toward that.

Sometimes, it is difficult to believe that we can release the discordant and inept aspects of our character, that we can dismiss them like an old coat and be new, but we can, by: embodying the living force in our daily lives in every experience, not allowing our old character to drive us, and being driven only by our *inner knowing self*'s inspirations in our heart, knowing that what we wish in our spiritual consciousness is our personal truth and *will* come to pass.

We *learn* to believe. Incorporating belief comes with discipline. We *develop* compassion, energy, and spiritual reasoning through a program of daily ritual. Through continued devotion, day in and day out, to living from our spiritual Self's perceptions, we can become better able to reconstruct our foibles and successfully analyze our whole potential existence.

When we open ourselves to frequenting the inner place of harmony, we develop a familiarity with that Energy—until nothing else is real to us except the most necessary belief that we are able to fully express our spiritual Self in our life. Even if we forget how to be in harmony, we are able to recover the procedure with this potent attitude:

Let me live in harmony with all of life.

Instilling this attitude in our every breath, infusing this attitude in our every moment, embracing this attitude in our every encounter and every action, alters our experiences to feeling totally at-one with life's glorious aspects.

The most significant lesson we learn on the inner pathway is to believe in ourselves regardless of disillusionment. When we endeavor to harmonize, we reap the reward of feeling at peace, and nothing can discourage us.

The Presence is a powerful concept we learn to engage as a force of mind and action. When we decide to live from the strength of our spirit, we open our awareness to a multitude of options, which includes embracing what before threatened or frightened us. We courageously devote ourselves to overcoming the qualities and circumstances we may have felt were destructive. We learn to be strong through the energy and awareness of our spiritual Nature, to know that we can overcome the personality weaknesses that have burdened us.

The time comes when we no longer function as we did and the only reality we know is the one blossoming within us and spreading itself out about us—like the new earth—born from our innate sweetness and born from our courage.

Spiritual discipline is the crux of the new society, discipline to vitalizing the whole Self, because it takes consistency of action to be a new human. Discipline in habits and in practicing the attunement reaches into our psyche and changes the metabolic structure of our body. Discipline of viewpoints and words alters our experience with others and restructures our personality's secrets; which open, unfold, heal, and dry up ... and we recover.

When we focus on resynergizing hope in our endeavors, and we hold to that hope with every fiber of our being, what we aim toward and move toward regularly begins to shape into the very reality we have sought. We are capable of accomplishing our heartfelt goals. Continuity of belief takes us there.

By our actions and attitudes, most significantly we create the world in which we live. The way we experience life is an expression of our innermost process. How we view the circumstances in which we live—endeavors, relationships, and their tenor—reflects our ability to fully live from our potent Character. When we diligently pursue what we know is our best choice, we find it, because our inner being cries to be heard and to be given its fullest expansion of opportunity.

Everything humanity wishes to be is now shaping within us individually. In our inner lives, we are maturing abundantly. We are becoming intuitively discerning and powerfully able to visualize and manifest. In our outer lives, we are practicing making these truths apparent in our reality—until life will become exactly what we have envisioned.

> *It is imperative to hold to your vision and to know it is your truth.*

To alter humanity's total experience, we alter our own experience. The consequences eventually will manifest for the whole, because what we are the world is.

10

Our New Attitude

In the basic training of our psyche, we learn to embody the full capacity of our spiritual being. We drink in our divine Nature. We engage the Divine Mind. We blink with the Mind through the consciousness of our soul's presence, which itself is a living force distinct from our personality.

To relinquish your unknowing self and embrace continuously your powerful Identity:

- Open your heart and mind, and define life by the Universal Powers that guide you.

- Believe that those Powers illuminate your existence, and realign your focus toward a higher cause and purpose.

- Live the laws of nature to the best of your ability every day.

- Stop playing games of self-doubt, self-judgment, and "woe is me."

- Responsibly share with others what wisdom you learn.

- Learn to believe in the Unseen Presences who give you their counsel and train you in your exquisite capacities as a spiritual being, to be used as a vehicle for life.

On the path of deepening awareness:

- Release all conditions that have blocked your happiness.

- Forgive every individual who has saddened your experience.

- Participate in activities that lift your sense of well-being.

- Gently applaud your insights.

- Courageously venture forth in the hope of acquiring serenity.

- Acquire knowledge as a tool of the Divine.

- Listen to the powerful quiet *voice* within you.

Following these criteria leads us to a quiet yet profound perception of our own unique capacity to be whole, majestic, and extraordinarily happy. We heal our soul wounds and learn self-affection, self-love, and courage. We discover the Unseen Constituents who are our guiding lights.

All of society is reconstructing. We are renewing our links with each other and with our spiritual Selves. We are rising into a greater synchronicity with the forces of existence, in ways we have yet to ascertain. For the good of all and our own satisfaction, humanity is acquiring a state of being that will encompass holiness.

It is possible to heal the wounds of our psyche. We are capable of behavior modifications that can teach us compassion and bring us into a new form of living. Nothing is more powerful in this world than our mind in sync with our innate divine Self.

Humanity is rising. We will forget the anguish and no longer subject ourselves to dismay and struggle. The day will come when we will have learned a greater focus of existence. That greater focus is compassion for ourselves and each other. Life will reflect our innate loveliness. We will exemplify the flawless Nature with which we were born.

We did not come into life subject to a God who desires to control or frighten us. We did not come into life with inhibitions. We did not come into life with restraints upon our spirit. We grew these ... and we can undo them. We can undo our suffering.

The greatest healer—the natural state of our being—is to love one another, despite our distinctions. To love one another, despite our fears. To love one another with all of the will within us for something better. As we do, we are raised in our vision and begin to heal our pasts.

11

Our New Heart

The era we are entering will bring a psychological breakthrough for all of humanity. It is a serendipitous moment in the infinite spirit of humankind.

This extraordinary experience we are exploring together is consciousness expansion, and consciousness is not mental but is of the heart. Consciousness is that place in the whole Self that is open to surrendering judgment and fear, willing to cooperate and find a middle ground of understanding. Consciousness is the breadth of our whole being, the center of our being, our spiritual Nature. Consciousness is *us* without fear, remorse, anxiety, or judgment.

Until we learn to live in grace and composure, we are surrounded by discomfort and we strive to relinquish the animosity that suffocates us. This becomes a powerful exercise because, while we desire to achieve a higher presence and to envision our potential, we also are recovering from many lifetimes of suffering. This latter component has shaped the human personality more than dissension or astrological influences.

The essential Personality of our spiritual Nature comprises the criteria by which we evolve. When we are aggressive, our spiritual Self suffers. When we are generous and we resonate with a fresh acceptance of beauty, our spiritual Self is unafraid and realizes a kinship with others. When we are free of disgust, our life is harmonious. The equilibrium of our consciousness depends on the degree of love we invoke from our deep, eternal, and divine Personality.

In the overview of human consciousness, it is quite acceptable to devise strategies by which to unlock our innate inner goodness and to embrace the naturally spontaneous spirit we are. When we do, we complement the esoteric side of life from which come the visionary talents that give us direction and create a yearning to live wholly. This formidable situation imposes itself on our behaviors, until we become critically involved with the spiritual frequencies and we simplify our life to a more harmonious existence.

Having an open heart is one of the most necessary characteristics we develop as we rise into the new energy, because until we are able to look upon others with humility and we honor their presence, we have learned nothing of any real value for our own growth. When we ourselves judge any other, we are judged. Love is the natural human state. Freely expressing our inclination to forgive and to understand the frailties of human nature does us much good.

Certainly, sometimes any of us may have a good reason to feel angry or pained over another person's actions. Yet how can we live if all we think about is our anger and pain? How can we move forward if we are unable to let go of that bondage that ties us to our past? Rather, let go, accept what is, and resolve to be a better person for it.

Most significantly, we of humanity are learning respect. We are learning that the highest good of all depends on each of us living in harmony. The human race is evolving to its full potential by each of us who is striving to be a better person and is contributing to the betterment of society.

By each person who is helping to heal the planet and better influence the children (who are conscious, aware, and present in the light of divine understanding), the human race is acquiring a new awareness and perspective for how to heal the earth and the problems that have plagued us. The human race will survive because we are improving our social patterns and learning to cooperate with people we do not understand.

Compassion is the resolve needed to correct the ills of society. With compassion, we are able to imagine alternatives and we are lifted into the joyous possibilities of a global vision that can seed a world that is balanced and carefree.

The true measure of whether we are accomplishing our goals is our willing application of the principles by which we live in our mind. Living from our heart with a clarity of purpose, understanding, and compassion improves our life immediately.

12

Our New Perceptions

When in our spiritual level of perception, we do not get upset. We are not persuaded to be angry. We do not feel disturbed. We have learned ways to deal with these emotions. This is humanity's future.

When we use our inner wisdom, we can live tranquilly without feeling shaken by circumstances, because we remain *still* in the eye of the storm. We feel calm and at peace and unwilling to lose our position of harmony, even if we are in error or inadvertently caused a disturbance. In the flow of the inner reality, we trust that everything will unfold appropriately and without undue distress.

These are the features that will most create the new society. With these qualities in our feelings and behaviors, we are not afraid of what will become of us. We walk through the shadows of the world without flinching. We release and commit to remain in our peaceful state of mind. We decide we are unwilling to be angry. We even forget what it is like to be angry. We measurably learn not to be upset over what previously would have upset us. Even though by rights we may be entitled to be upset, we are not, which makes our life much easier.

When we relinquish control of our life to a peace-loving focus, we no longer denounce others because we remember that we also err. Others may be frustrated when we are not angry, resistant or reluctant, but we remain calm and clear by our decision and choice to remain so.

Such a state of mind is a primary facility of the spiritual consciousness. The precious beliefs that humanity will cherish in the new society will bid us all toward a calm and clear presence of mind in all circumstances. We will acquire the passion of complementing others. We will fully appreciate our relationships, viewing them as opportunities to temper a kind nature in us. We will see others as expressions of our own self and realize that each relationship reflects our evolving Self.

When we perceive others as essential components of our sensitivity training, we see them in a clear and enhanced light rather than judge them. We accept that we have a personal liaison with them because of what we both can learn during the time shared. This attitude releases the stranglehold of our expectations, and we comprehend that each relationship is a free expression of mutual beliefs and needs.

As we wean ourselves from harmful dependencies, characteristically we decide to let go of controlling the outcomes of our encounters. Uniquely, we prefer relationships that fulfill our need to be aligned spiritually, mentally, and emotionally. When complemented by people who fairly estimate and challenge our attitudes and behaviors, we reason even more astutely.

Ultimately, this will prove to be the most powerful technique to polish humanity's senses as expanding Selves, because relationships hone us in a way that is not possible otherwise. With this clear understanding, we better appreciate our relationships. We evaluate new encounters not for what we desire from them but for the esoteric implications they have toward helping us shape our own true Self.

In the times ahead, we will be resistant only for as long as we feel angry. We will no longer perceive others falsely, because we will no longer admonish ourselves for our disillusionments and frustrations. If we do inwardly refuse to take charge of our own life, hoping someone else will lift us out of our misery, it will be because we are afraid of fully expressing our spiritual power ... although that is not possible and, no matter how it seems, it cannot be.

We have the power to change our personal point of view regarding self-enhancement, self-appreciation, and self-love. Understanding these qualities is when we alter the course of our life. That is when the path we follow reaches a turning point and we see choices that previously we could not imagine.

Then, in a very clearly defined process, we distinctly comprehend who we are. We no longer resist our soul's awareness that is struggling to rise into our waking consciousness. We no longer fear the precious insights that guide, protect, and inspire us. We see that our experiences are a doorway to our whole Self. We realize that every experience strengthens us in some way. Thus, we become more attuned to the spiritual being we are.

Coming to terms with our personal strength and compassion is why we are in life, a reason we are physical, a reason we explore how to be more of the person we feel we can be. It is truly fortunate when we begin to see that life is a fabrication of our soul's needs and is not an unavoidable kink around which we must move. Once we take hold of each encounter with an outlook of self-realization, through an exchange of ideas and energy, we heal the discrepancies in our character that have blocked our self-esteem.

In our lives that are filled with interactions and experiences of a physical nature, sometimes we overlook the importance of our spiritual Self's viewpoint. However, once we evaluate each moment as an opportunity, we become more attuned to the synchronicities of life and open-minded to what might develop.

What is our inner voice's relationship to the conditions in the world? The inner counselor is more precious in our whole experience than living in the framework called "instinctive." Being able to advise ourselves from the inner wisdom is supra-intelligent, supra-instinctual, and is beyond personal experience. It surpasses any logical alternative.

Inner reality perceptions can heal personal social dysfunctions effectively; in fact, can clarify our emotions and strengthen our sensitivities so that we are less gullible and more aware.

Consequently, when we envision ourselves in comparatively friendly circumstances with people we trust, not only are we able to perceive through the usual senses but we are able to invoke a clarity of understanding that amplifies all possible premises upon which to base our decisions.

For a joyful and sane life and personal survival, it is critical to connect with our *inner knowing self*'s clear counsel. By aligning with that point of view in our life and relationships, we learn to attract blessings rather than distresses. We value ourselves as inherently spiritual. To others, we communicate as a person vested with sensitivity, compassion, and enlightenment. We realize it is our inner Self who is living the physical life; our inner Self who is experiencing the world, learning from the world, and giving to the world; our inner Self who is the student of life and our teacher.

To align with your most viable Character and tap the core of your being, your essential Self, focus on creating harmony and alleviating dissonance. Focus on healing misunderstandings and invoking the perceptions of your kinder, attuned Self.

13

Finding Our Tolerance

Our inner Self fashions our choices and decisions from a higher perspective about how we may best develop the qualities of our true Character. This is best defined as conscience in control.

The true conscience is the voice of our spiritual Self, not the subconscious recordings from our childhood. When we are attuned to being useful to others and grateful for each day that we exist, our conscience is the voice of God. A clear conscience is the *still, soft inner voice* that guides us with love and patience. However, when we are not aligned with the qualities of our true being, we are more absorbed in daily dramas and how to fix the problems that we feel overwhelm our lives.

Much more pleasant, and no more difficult, is focusing on our inner being as the model of character we can and must be, and to live that Character consciously every day to the best of our ability.

When we purposely seek the freedom that comes from a clear mind and clear heart, our attitude is to give-give-give of our truth, our clarity, and our assessment as a spiritually centered person. Such an attitude restores self-esteem and heals the feeling of being separate from others. With such an attitude, we realize that we need others to feel connected to life. Without that connection, we may feel as if we are floundering without a purpose, goal, or reason for being, which is the focal point that directs our actions in life.

When open to living based on kindness and goodwill, we can forgive ourselves and others. This attitude is an essential functioning trait for our psyche, after which a willingness to explore other ways of being blessed evolves in our mental development. For example, can we forgive ourselves and others for their or our tragedies wrought in an unconscious state?

We are each responsible for our own actions, and we each know what amends we must make. That is a part of spiritual learning, of becoming strong and reasoning toward living more usefully.

To forgive yourself:

- Live the new attitudes to the best of your ability.

- Focus not on anger or anguish.

- Focus on healing your fears and conditioned reflexes.

How can we forgive others for their despicable beliefs and judgments against us? How can we forgive people for their reflexes that have caused us pain or suffering? How can we forgive people whose great venomous behaviors have changed our lives? In our heart—for our *own* peace.

When in moments of alignment, we are free of judgment. We see that every person has the inner counselor available. We see their struggle to acquire balance, yet their inability to imagine or comprehend their spiritual power; consequently, they reach beyond themselves with a destructive vibration.

When another person causes you harm—physical or psychological, distinguish between that person's actions, behaviors, and attitudes from the *soul self* beneath that is struggling to survive. Strive to understand that person's pain while, at the same time, act responsibly toward his or her irresponsible actions. For example, in the same way that we might take a child who has misbehaved, reprimand that child and set a condition for recompense without ourselves feeling angry, so we can with people who have separated themselves from the group consciousness and from their own divine Nature.

In this world of many peoples, while individual identity is valued and worthy, none of us would exist if others were not in the world with us. The primary purpose of aligning to our spiritual being is to recognize that every person is linked with all others, regardless of demeanors, beliefs, appearances, or judgments.

On the inner level, every person is a part of a group consciousness that moves as one in the *Void* and breathes as one being. The inner Self focuses attention on lifestyles. The inner Self has a presence of mind that enhances life for the whole.

People who do not live this way do not yet perceive their true Nature or Character and do not fathom their link with others. They separate themselves from the whole by their lack of attunement to the goodness that is within them.

The inner voice is unequivocally the power of the world, the source of wisdom, and the inner teacher for actions that bring joy, heal pain, and free us from ambivalence and uncertainty. Every person on Earth has the inner voice, whether or not they heed it.

People who acknowledge this divine inner voice live a life of concerted effort to being useful, kind, and compassionate. People who deny or ignore the voice are separating themselves from the Divine. As long as they refuse to heed the innate kindness of their own soul, they become even more disconnected. Pity them, help them, forgive them.

This does not mean allow or tolerate any wrongdoing. It means take firm action, but without bludgeoning them with a cruel heart. They do not yet appreciate their responsibility to the whole.

Our task only is to uphold the whole of goodness. The point of view is to respect, appreciate, and honor others.

14

Finding Our Virtue

We want peaceful relationships. We want life to flow happily and freely. Yet such a life seems uncommon. What can you do to kindle the flame of hope?

- Inspire yourself with the concept that you are capable of resolving differences and negotiating harmony.

- Strive to understand why other people feel differently, why your attitudes and viewpoints are at odds, and accept that.

- Reach a peace *for* others, even if only in your own heart.

- Ascertain your own values and primary needs.

- Reconstruct your own patterns of behavior in your relationships and your place in society.

- Reassess who *you* are, why *you* live, and what *you* can do to help others.

We are unlimited in our capacity to heal the scars of our psyche. In the times ahead, humanity will be fond of sanctity and virtue, which mirror our essential good Self. Foremost, we will appreciate consideration of people's feelings and needs. By living these attitudes, we will step into a new co-existence. We will see others as our equals. We will overcome our enemy, which is ourselves.

What the world is we are, and what we are the world becomes. Everything we admire about life and social interaction begins *within* as a model of behavior and speech.

To know the purpose of your existence and to know great satisfaction:

- Connect with your spiritual awareness.

- Fuel your imagination.

- Go forward with a new vision of your abilities and a new hope for your future.

For strength of character:

- Coalesce your innermost needs into a single concentration; to support yourself as well as others with compassion, insight, and a serendipitous inclination. As you do, you begin to plant new possibilities that will build the new society.

- Simplify your interactions into a comprehensive, lovely strategy for resolving your differences, anguished cries, and painful memories.

- Live for harmony, and anticipate that harmony is possible. Expect harmony and it will be your truth. Engage this vision daily.

- Comprehend the meaning of your existence by fraternizing with the Higher Realms of life.

- Heighten your dreams.

- Enhance your capacity to understand.

- Open your heart.

We humans are compassionate beings. When we open our minds to the possibility that we are capable of living from our spiritual Nature, that becomes our truth.

Society is not peaceful today, but we can engineer that result— by resuming *stature* as the model for our being and *quiescence* as the model for our lives. We can turn society around by learning to transcend our fears and worries and to change our viewpoint to living from our innate sweetness.

15

Finding Our Spiritual Self

When life experiences become extremely stressful, we investigate finer reasons for being. We conclude, after searching, that life is more than physical.

The following principles best characterize a spiritual life: astute perceptions about all aspects of experience, an inclination toward matters of the inner Self, a forgiving Nature, a generous character, and being a living example of kindness.

By living these segments of our true Personality, we are better able to visualize our strength and to embody these qualities in our everyday character. When our main concern is how to be a person of such repute, we begin the arduous task of self-clarifying what we perceive to be necessary for living our own truth. We reach a point of no longer feeling the hand of sadness on our brow. Rather, we feel renewed daily through the spirit of the inner kingdom and embraced daily by the spirit of the Universal Mind, or God.

If you are inclined toward the lifestyle of living from your Presence and friendship with the Light, and to fully embodying the life principles you have learned to value, what behaviors guide your life?

How do you make choices and decisions?

- Live with an aspiration toward fairmindedness and responsibility for your life.

- Strive to be an example of the highest resolute being imaginable.

- Live according to the universal truth in you, regardless of how circumstances appear to be.

- Value other people's opinions as insightful and practical, as measures to guide your own vision toward the fundamental principles of action for a fulfilling life.

- Sympathize with, acknowledge, and incorporate the shadow side of life—not allowing it to enforce its viewpoint, but controlling it (rather than denying it) by your choice of spiritual consciousness in action.

- Breathe in the *cosmic fire,* the prana that saturates all living things. Breathe it in as the very sustenance of your eternal mind and spirit. Breathe it in as the essential fabric of your wholeness, that tangible yet ephemeral substance that links us to all things and all matter.

- Admire the higher sensitivities that alleviate distresses and irrational inhibitions.

- Open to the power of the universe in your heart and mind, and willfully engage in intelligent and insightful occupational pursuits.

- Value and hold in high esteem the opportunities that abound around you for following the path of higher will.

- Join with all spiritual persons who endeavor to awaken the light within, those who are sincere and devoted to all that is good.

- Favor the ability to envision beauty and to comply, with all speed, with those visionary trustees who plant beauty in the world. Add your own vision to the whole and live your own life in that regard.

- Achieve synchronicity and compliance with the Divine Presence in your interactions every day.

Our happiest moments are in our agreements with others; wherein bliss infuses us, tranquility fills us, and we are at peace. When we embody the living principles of the Divine—which we feel and know in the center of our being—we measure the choices of our life by them. For example, you choose:

- Synchronicity as your lifestyle, those seeming miraculous and apparent coincidental events that are natural occurrences in life and are recognized by remaining mentally alert and openly aware of the larger picture of the tapestry of life that connects us all.

- Full awareness as a higher thinking Self, aware of your innate ability to comprehend the abstract processes of living.

- Actualizing solutions to problems through inner wisdom and the guiding instincts of your *inner knowing self.*

- Responsibility because its value is a form of self-discipline toward self-reliance and self-approval.

- Abiding by what represents value to all persons and all living beings, because every person is a member of the human species and a member of the Consciousness manifest.

- Acting each day as your spirit wills you and guides you, because the inner Self is the living body of God.

- Achieving wondrous things and striving toward wondrous accomplishments, because that is the drive of the Omnipotent within us—to stretch itself to be more than it has been.

- Admiring and reaching through your heart toward all that you know is your innate ability to be.

- Expanding in every way possible that your heart inspires you.

- Lifting up your beliefs into the realm of knowing that what your heart moves you to pursue is more than a foolish dream and more than for self alone. That it is essential to the very existence of all life and to the evolution of all that is holy. That your personal presence and inspiration are a part of that vast movement of the consciousness of the whole, and your own energy and light are needed to keep that *force* active and vital as you ascend into a new identity and individual form of thought and being.

- Accepting that your devotion to your inner promptings and inner guide is worthy and necessary; because it is the Spirit of Life prodding you into realms uncertain and untapped, urging you to explore, investigate and give all that you are, regardless of how unusual you may believe your talents are. This is your destiny and your gift to the world.

- Trusting that the Universe guides you fairly and that—when you devote your heart and whole being to consciously living the natural laws and applying yourself in every way to acting out the principles that guide you—your efforts will bear fruit.

These are the steps to the precious potency and to embracing God. We make these choices as we step toward a life of inner tranquility.

When we live consciously, with the voice of life as our conscience, we are unafraid. We believe in the power that invests us with a vision to understand and to apply masterfully all that we feel guided to contribute to the lives and consciousness of others. We value the visions that move through us. We value the wisdom innate in every soul. We know that every person carries the Divine Presence within and that our own viewpoint is no more and no less remarkable.

Everything we are is a part of the greater good of life. Everything we are is an extension of the whole of life. When we daily invest our whole Self—body, mind, and spirit—with whatever techniques, processes, or rituals enable us to tap the *center* of our being, we reinstill our spiritual alignment. We reach out to others. We take the hands that guide us, teach us, and hold us. All around us are teachers and friends willing to be there for us when we open our heart to them.

The following components help us to invoke spiritual splendor as a daily "food." These qualities are invaluable for visualizing our potential and clarifying our inner strength:

- *Perfectly blending with others.* When we realize that the presence of others affects us, we visualize a greater strength within ourselves.

- *Living with curiosity and enjoyment, like a child.* This clarifies our sensitivity to our purpose in life.

- *Appreciating all that comes to us.* When attuned to the serendipitous occurrences in life, simultaneously we become free through the auspicious powers inherent in our being.

The following characteristics align you with your divine purpose:

- Counsel yourself and others with a vision of wholeness and a capacity to bridge the vast range of talents that are innate in your whole Self.

- Visually resonate to living a higher consciousness lifestyle, which daily reinforces that you live sensitively to the magnificent opportunities that abound around you.

- Alleviate your discomfort and kindle your hope by learning to be self-empowered.

- Dedicate to yourself and others—in all that you do—the unique gifts of spirit with which you are blessed.

These characteristics are the essential diet of a successful spiritual life. When we live each day for the highest good of all, we are filled with light.

16

Our New Mind

Part of becoming a new human is in evolving mentally. We develop the newer visionary style by awakening our spiritual consciousness and our precious self-esteem. This is the primary need facing humanity today because, until we closely analyze and strengthen our connection with our *inner knowing self,* we are nothing more than a body aware of being human. However, once we identify that we are a spirit in a body, we coordinate the activities of our life to be spiritual as well as physical.

Everything we express as a physical being becomes extraordinarily simple because, once we analyze our nature as an evolving spiritual being, we are no longer unsure of who we are. We define our precious life as an opportunity to learn more about our spirit, which aligns us and clears our thoughts. Our life then becomes truly successful, with quality and meaning in our innermost sacred accomplishments. Even recognition does not affect our decisions. When aligned mentally and devoted to the principles of life that guide us, nothing of this world can sway us. Our thoughts are shaped by our beliefs in higher thought.

We awaken the *delight* through understanding the significance of being mentally attuned to the Divine that guides us in everyday activities. When filled with a clear appreciation of the inner counselor, our day-to-day actions become harmonious and without anticipation or anxiety. Rather, we live to be appreciated only for our sanctified actions. All else becomes irrelevant.

When imbued with the spiritual frequencies of thought and intuition, we are sedate in our manner and speech. We do not appeal for recognition or seek appreciation. We are not anxious about whether we will be understood. We are not confused about the various feelings that define conscious living. We are not unsure of our actions. With a sense of blessing, we calmly decide to activate the natural thinking processes that are a blend of the Universal Mind with our own innermost sacred Self. In strategizing the potential union with our spiritual Self, we attain precise visions and interpretations of cosmic delight. We feel at-one and begin to live this practically with others.

Using these criteria, we evaluate our own processes when we are not at-one with the Universal Mind because, when synergizing the thinking process with our inner counselor's vision, we are advancing as a soul in a physical body.

Being human has a range of possibilities. First, we attain the clear vision toward which we have aspired for many eons. We recognize the state of mind called God. We are attracted to the spiritual being we will become.

Once open to this system of interpretation, our clarity and distinctive focus come into play and hope enforces within us inner promptings to live from our light.

17

Our New Body

The new reality is taking over one person at a time in our changing perceptions and attitudes. The new world will take over individually long before everyone on Earth will transform. That is why it is important to identify how we evolve into the lighter frequency physical body.

Who we are constitutes not only our personal thoughts but also our physical form. The human body frequently refines; changing shape, density, appearance, and health. Scientists say that the cells of the body completely change every seven years. Beyond the effect of basic genetic makeup and mental habits, at this time in human history, the human body is in transition to its next evolutionary stage.

Material existence operates on different levels of frequency. Some frequencies, or degrees of vibration, are more dense, such as ice; others may be less dense, such as water, vapor, or air. In a similar way, the physical body is changing its level of vibratory frequency to a more refined degree.

There are some significant differences between the current third-dimension physical body, the one most humans have now, and the new higher vibrational physical body, which results from living the new awareness. Both forms decay, but the newer body decays more slowly; for a longer period of time, the higher frequency body resists destroying vibrations (disease) that cause disintegration.

Over time, it will become obvious to humanity that the body's disintegration results from personality dysfunction(s), self-disillusionment, and/or a fascination for destroying habits and attitudes. Essentially, physical disintegration results from foolish behaviors and choices.

Our most foolish belief, says the Divine Mind, and perhaps the most destructive on our health, is accepting that we cannot reach and live from the sensitivity of our spiritual consciousness. Foolishness is believing that we function independently of others, cannot show responsibility without becoming absorbed by others' demands, must be controlling to avoid losing ourselves, and regard ourselves as a failure—however, we only fail when we no longer try, says the Divine Mind.

Humanity's higher purpose is to invoke spiritual consciousness by how we take care of our body. Alignment with our inner Self invokes wellness.

In the new human body, ideally we consume higher force foods that uplift us physically as well as mentally (e.g., *live* foods such as blue-green algae, sprouts, vegetables, and fruits that have not been depleted of their natural abundance of vitamins, minerals, and enzymes).

The reason is that biologically the body is an energy field and the foods we eat are energy. When we consume foods that are impure, we are depleting the energy source that keeps the body functioning efficiently. Because the body is organic, it needs proper fuel in much the same way that machines need proper care (e.g., cars, computers). Improper fuel "gums up" the body's operation, clogs the "pipelines," and corrodes the tissues.

In the times ahead, humanity will desire to function mentally at an optimum potential, and we will realize that certain foods affect our ability to think clearly.

To acquire a more clear consciousness, one of the first elements we learn to discern is what to eat for our own body and chemistry, which we do by observing how our body feels and reacts to particular foods. If a food causes us to feel disgruntled or to dislike ourself, it is a negative effect beginning to destroy the brain cells; disease continues from there. To feel aligned with our spiritual power and not overwhelmed by the forces of life, we eat for consciousness.

What foods are beneficial and what foods are harmful to your own individual body?

When you feel flushed with an increased level of energy, the food you are eating is giving you strength. When you feel a creative burst of awareness while eating and are stimulated mentally, you are eating a food of higher causative force. When you feel energized by what you eat and move quickly through the meal, to get on with your focus of the day, that food is a productive vibrational stimulation. Any time you are consciously aware of synthesis mentally and emotionally and your body feels invigorated, that food is supporting your spiritual consciousness.

The other side is foods that dampen the spirit. While eating, if you feel tired, sleepy, disgruntled, uncomfortable, confused, or dysfunctional, that food is unclear or unproductive for maintaining a higher energy field and ideal physical body. Such a food may not affect someone else negatively, but may affect your unique chemistry or sensitivity. This applies to any food that causes a disagreeable reaction in the body, emotions, or mental clarity.

Foods that cause you to feel out of sorts, unsettled, angry, impatient, or frustrated, are foods that stimulate the lower energy field. Any symptoms that are immediate or within an hour after eating—such as disorientation, loss of power, dismay, or discouragement—indicate that you have eaten something that lowers your concentration and, thereby, deters your energy level. Any symptoms, such as feeling disturbed or ambivalent, complicate the state of wellness. It is recommended that we completely avoid such foods.

If you strangle, gag or choke while eating, or soon after, your body is rejecting a food and it is wise to discontinue eating it altogether. Any sensation in the body, in any part of the body, while eating or within the first hour after eating, indicates a food allergy that is uncomfortable, at least, and may be destructive. What may begin as a mild reaction, if the food is ingested regularly can become quite serious; such a food is best avoided for an extended time, says the Divine Mind, such as one year, to allow the body to heal and gain new strength before experimenting with that food again. In some cases, the food may be reabsorbed, or you may never be able to tolerate it.

Consuming lower vibrational foods does not nurture our spiritual power. We are advised to choose foods that are filled with the force of life, such as fresh herbs from a garden and vegetables that have not been overcooked or tainted by toxins.

Also recommended is fewer, minimal, or no meats. Such a program gives us the ability to think clearly, feel physically powerful and vitalized, and emotionally in harmony and at peace. These are general answers, yet provide a comfortable lifestyle, says the Divine Mind.

Sometimes, we humans abuse the body. When this affects our happiness, it is devastating and even critical to our life span. It is significantly even more so with the new higher vibrational body. Not only is that body overwhelmed physically, but at the very least we also lose the ability to perceive from the higher awareness. We also may lose clear comprehension of our life purpose and life direction.

It is very precious, therefore, to realize that we need a well physical body in order to activate most effectively the new level of vibration on Earth. When our body is not functioning in its purest state possible, we are not able to tolerate the energy shifts without feeling the "uplifting" as a force preventing us from evolving. Our actions and attitudes in the new direction then feel like a weight holding us back.

Interestingly, when we assume a personality shift, by centering on the divine *inner knowing,* causatively we also affect others. So, how we view ourselves and others closely attunes with the principles we learn to appreciate in our newer vision of prosperous thinking and living.

It is essential, therefore, to visualize ourselves as whole and to live accordingly—by our inner knowing characteristics that elevate our desires and yearnings to eat well and live harmoniously.

To live wholly, with peace of mind and delight:

- Realize that every encounter serves as a form of motivation toward your goals.

- Surrender your needs to your *inner knowing self*'s inherent characteristics and desires.

- Live in humility, to show that you value others.

- Comprehend your place in life.

- Reach out for understanding.

- Understand that you causatively affect the world around you by your choices and actions.

- Formulate a plan of action that reflects your divine being and purpose.

- Visualize your capacity to be more tolerant.

- Concertedly apply your whole experience of the moment toward fully endowing others through your generosity of spirit and being.

- Value every moment of your life.

- Utilize all of your experiences as a "voice" for your future needs.

By allowing our spiritual Self to fill us, we are more confident and we absorb the necessary listening qualities for being aware of the universal powers that impact us every day.

To go forward with a new consciousness and reasoning power, forgive your blunders and allow your *inner knowing self*'s values to clear the way for what you do in life.

To illuminate your new being and body, live in your powerful Presence at all times and express that focus through your decisions and actions.

To bear fruit, live your whole truth, lift into your highest capacity of forgiveness, and listen to the guiding force in your heart for why you were born.

To embrace your new and more complete Self, attend to your physical being.

18

Finding Our Compassion

The Divine Mind says that earthquakes, floods, and tidal waves will increase during the 21st century. If that is true, how do we acquire and exude tranquility?

Compassion heals a worrying nature, a compassion for all of our struggles. As we grow in the capacity to be affectionate and loving toward all, we learn compassion, which is the depth of our spirit.

To acquire compassion:

- Linger daily in your spiritual Identity.

- Spend time courting your spiritual Persona, until it takes over in your attitudes and actions.

- Live by the principles of powerful inner direction, which may motivate you to be compassionate and able to heal all your strife.

- Listen from your *inner knowing self.*

- Adhere to your inner counselor's advice.

- Determine that you are "musically" sensitized to all vibrations and sounds, and acquire higher senses to engage the tones of majestic expression.

- Engage the Supreme Mind's energy force as your own dear wisdom, through which you surround yourself with a force field of protection against all catastrophic conditions, events, and circumstances.

- Free your expectations and do not compromise with any person regarding the advice of your *inner knowing self.* Listen only to your inner counselor when faced with ridicule or objection. Devote yourself to your inner counselor's wise direction for your existence.

- Do not engage in, pursue, or allow in your contemplations any practice or endeavor that is not in harmony with your own experience. If you sometimes admonish yourself or others for indiscretions, this is of little importance overall. Of greater value—for acquiring the inner power—is to subject yourself truthfully to the ways of harmony you see before you.

- Awaken sensitivity to your spiritual Identity, through which you may seed conceptual perceptions and a lack of bias and judgment. This clears a path through your psyche—beyond distresses and fears—into the clear space of your inner being.

- Discover your capacity for forgiveness, hope and understanding. Be willing to leave behind what has burdened you. In this way, you are no longer overcome by all with which you have struggled, you no longer judge your present by your past, and you are no longer afraid to surrender to the power of the Universal Light that you sense guides you.

- Begin to drop behaviors that are not your true Self. Exist solely within the protection of a kind demeanor and a sincere devotion to being thoughtful, courageous, and forthright.

- Flow with appropriate actions effortlessly and without preconception. Concentrate and focus through your *inner knowing self,* even if you are still frequently perplexed.

- Believe in your potential extraordinary capacity for being wholly at-one with your quiescent Self and devoted to what you identify as God.

- Find life amusing, with an attitude of delight and childlike whimsy that flows through you like a gentle summer breeze, passes beyond you like the fragrance of summer lilies, and gently surrounds and caresses all of life that you touch by your presence.

- Become amazed at the wonders of life, at the intricacies of the power, and at the brilliant fascinations you have had for acquiring intellectual pursuits; amazed at the quandaries you have allowed yourself to fall into by a lack of insight and amazed at your capacity for anguish.

- Learn that, indeed, you can be *still* in the midst of all around you. You can be *quiet* in the midst of fear and confusion. You can be so aligned that you are truly devoted to the inner power that guides you. In this way, serendipitously you encounter life, embrace every person, and joyously expect that all you do and all you hope for, indeed, will be fortuitous for everyone.

- You no longer hope only for your own sanctity. You hope for the sanctity of all living forms. You breathe serenity as your power increases, and devote yourself to fully integrating a joyous state of being.

- At this point, you begin to tap the core of your being, thereby realizing your capacity for being compassionate toward all persons and circumstances.

When we live compassionately, we are not devoured by necessity or desire. We walk in the midst of despair and it touches us not. We live from an attitude of oneness with the Cosmic Consciousness guiding us. In our complete Stature, we are at peace.

19

The Doorway

We access the center of our being by letting go of limiting what we believe is true. By releasing judgment, we open our heart to the inner voice, which offers us understanding.

The inner voice is the inner counselor that guides us on how to live well. When we deny the counsel of the *still, small inner voice,* we lose ourselves because, without that counsel, we wander aimlessly and have no grasp of how to be truly at peace.

Sometimes we are unable to perceive the inner voice because it speaks so softly. Sometimes we regress in our ability to live humanely, because it is our spiritual Nature that opens our viewpoint toward living in goodwill and fairmindedness. By relaxing our expectations, we become more gentle and thoughtful and we risk more to be happy.

To fill your own life with serenity, relax your guard against the unfolding of your softness.

Life is an opportunity to explore how to choose wisely, to evaluate our actions and reconstruct our attitudes. When social demands become less tolerable, increasingly we find ourselves in conflict.

At first, we extricate ourselves very slowly from the standards of visionless tyrants who seek to command us mentally and emotionally. Once we learn to walk away from delusions of grandeur and to seek the inner Presence, we find peace of mind. Once we integrate that Presence, we see with uncompromising insight.

By integrating, or fusing, our spiritual consciousness to our personality, we develop the ability to discern between right thought/right action and the mistaken powers of socially acceptable justice. As we exemplify this, we become truly effective, and only then. Judgments that once caused us grief dissolve. We even forget how to condemn others.

When we are full of the heavenly forces of life, nothing else but that guides our actions. Inherently, we observe the atrocities of this world with a centered knowing of their causes. This perception helps us to eliminate our own misguided behaviors and to comprehend the greater concepts of life. We even begin to like being human.

Being human is a limitation only when we forget that foremost we are a spiritual being. Being human is dangerous only when we have no sense of our whole being. Once we realize that our mind is our "heart" and our mind is our spirit, we train ourselves to utilize the full potential of our mind, which is cosmic. The mind is the vehicle through which we are given inspiration, vision, and insight. The mind awakens the inner voice.

Initially, feed your mind by stretching your capacity to imagine.

Through imagination, we tap the Cosmic Consciousness and lean upward toward our true Self, which is boundless. Mind is the expression of our true Self. Mind is our inner doorway to the higher realities and our soul.

When we train our mind to observe and listen to our inner senses and inner voice, we are invoking the Universal Thought Stream into our awareness, which then fills us with ideas that stretch our concepts of what is truth. So, we become able to envision a broader reality than we previously knew or understood.

Through the discipline of a clear mind, we touch the universal force called God. Through a disciplined and tutored mind, we hear the clear voice of God, which is soft and gentle.

The voice of the Divine is in everyone. When we train our mind to be *still,* we become able to perceive the small soft voice within us. With a still mind, we can connect with the Divine Presence in a very substantial way. Understanding comes when we are *still.*

To open your spiritual consciousness, concentrate on healing your mind. We heal our mind with prayer, meditation, the study of various spiritual teachings, and laughter!

Part III

Humanity's Heritage and Destiny

*The origin of the human species
and our splendid destiny.*

20

Humanity's Ancient Links

In the beginning of life on Earth, humanity already had existed elsewhere for many thousands of years, says the Divine Mind. Humanity did not originate on Earth. Our species began many, many eons ago, in another galaxy and on several other planets. We are not the only species in the universe, either. There are several varieties. Humanoid is predominant, but not at all singular in design.

Humanity originated in a universal layer called "etheric density." This was not the third dimension as we know it today, but at the time was the foremost example of how to manifest in a third-dimension reality.

For many, many eons in the original focus of being, humanoids were unable to procreate. They were not yet male and female, but were the first of their kind and devoted to their own existence. They came into being as a result of the development of materiality by a higher level of existence, which today we know as angels.

When exploring the original philosophies and inner wisdoms, we discover that the angels are more than we have imagined them to be. We learn they are a species of the Universal Consciousness, which, prior to the initial lifetimes in etheric matter, were not physical beings and held only light force and light energy, which is the angels' natural form.

This premise of existence is the original theory of how humans came to be, as recorded in the Akashic Records. In order to explore other elementary points of view in reality, some of the angels chose to materialize into a denser body of consciousness, which was multidimensional even then but had not yet been populated by higher intelligences.

This chapter identifies humanity's beginnings and how and why each of us is connected—at the very center of our being—to all other forms of life, because without the consciousness of life itself we would not be. Humanity is not central to existence, but is a fraction of it. There are many beings in many realities who carry the signature of the Divine Consciousness.

With evolutionary perceptions of reality, let us realize that the human species is one of many of its kind; humanoid meaning upright, intelligent, and filled with the breath of wisdom. Perhaps this information will become more valuable in humanity's self-estimation once we characterize ourselves as vehicles through which our higher evolved souls came into a third-dimension existence in order to purify their frequency vibrations of mind and spirit. Of course, this became necessary only after humanity began. Prior to that time, there were no mistakes in consciousness to warrant such a vehicle. However, since that time, one of the ways we humans evolve is through continuing realities in several lifetimes, both consecutively and in parallel.

When human lives began, we sought the fulfillment of spirituality. This became an obsession—until we forgot who we truly were and lost our inner connection to the total Presence. We obsessed over what we desired, and we forgot that we were already spiritual beings, although incarnate. This minor misunderstanding of what physical life was for led us down a path of ambivalence, misconception, and resistance to our inner knowing, which requires concentration and self-discipline. Therefore, we sought to acquire higher understanding.

Perhaps now humanity can realize that our greatest adventure lies in the inner realities, the dimensions that are within us. The inner worlds are far more fascinating in our perceptions of what is conducive to thought than the many outer worlds we see with our physical vision. In the inner worlds, we discover our power and compassion and, complementally, the voice of All That Is.

Following is the nature of the human species, as we align with other forms of life:

- We are capable of huge mistakes, yet just as capable of discovering incredible alternatives to any circumstance that arises.

- We are just as valid to each other as we are to the Higher Realms who postulate that we were once angels.

- We are able to impress upon our minds visionary strategies that illuminate our worthiness and compatibility. Once we reach the height of our sensory explosions and find the Void within us, we begin to comprehend the eternal spectrum of the All.

- We can become divine as a human being. When we are at our most clear, we are as near to divinity as the angels, says the Divine Mind.

- In all of our voices are the sounds of the universe in its wide ranges of musical tones of which our perceptions are but aspects. In the same way that rainbows reflect the various hues of reality, so our various tones reflect the spectrum of existence in vibration.

93

- Circumstances align our hopes and develop wisdom in us so that we may become honorable in our relationships to living in a world that is populated by millions of varieties of the Force, which we call the Divine Mind.

- Essentially, each one of us is a reflection of the most perfect Presence, which we name God.

- Living in a human form gives us an opportunity to appreciate the finer realities, within which all of the most cherished beings exist, including humans but not limited to humans.

- Suppose we created a species? How would we realize ourselves in it? Is it not perhaps the most extraordinary consideration to acknowledge that human beings are only one example of thousands of conscious life forms that have manifested to fulfill the integral aspects of the whole of life, or consciousness itself?

- Perhaps our humanoid form is but a capsule of the Life Presence so that it may experience itself in the subtler realities?

- Everything we of humanity have been able to conceptualize is but a droplet in the vast ocean of wisdom and experience. Our lives are unlimited because that of which we are a part is without boundary. Our lives represent the finest forms, which are, by definition, physical yet etheric.

We are not as individual as we seem. We are all bonded by an invisible web of the Life Presence. We are bound by that Presence, which, like an ocean, holds us as one breath and one body.

Our individual uniqueness is no more unique than a single perception is unique among all of our thoughts on any given day. We are so intricately connected to all living forms that each one of us is no more distinct in his or her originality than a single cactus is distinct from all other cacti in the desert.

We may appear divided. We may even think we are beyond devotion to others. Yet if we do not give our honor and humor in every action, attitude and manner, we are cutting the thread to our own existence, severing the link to our own support to that very existential quality of the Life Force that gives us meaning and the ability that we perceive as independent thought.

We are so integrally bound to all life forms that even our blood is a part of that same ocean of energy. Our individual shapes, colors, and sizes are like the various cells of a single organism. Our individuality helps us to convey most effectively our personal evolution of ideas and experiences. Yet, predominantly, all of us are able to visualize and telepathically communicate because of the symmetry of the life force in and through us.

The beginning of wisdom is the realization that there is no true individuality. Individuality is a fashionable interpretation of a Being we do not yet fully understand, a Being we all are compositely—the one we eternally identify as God.

The Divine Mind says that frequently we are re-evaluated by our Elders in the cosmic spectrum of the life forces. The human race, as a whole, is redefined genetically on occasion by the Peoples who originally seeded us here. This includes all various creative differences among us; because despite the differences we see, we are almost exactly identical to each other. We are certainly more identical to each other than to the human selves we were before we came to Earth.

We are all cells of a single Being named *Multiuniversal Self*. When we affirm that all beings, persons and animals, are common threads of one consciousness, we are allowing that every being is fully an extension of the same Divine Mind. We are living wholly in respect, because we realize that each being whom we call a living form represents the same universal power as we do. We no longer believe that our solitary consciousness is superior to any other form of life. We no longer think that our presence makes us better than any other. We understand that a composite of all life forms manifests the reality we live in and that, without each other, none of us would exist.

When attuning to the Universal Mind, we appreciate that the fragment of consciousness we call self is but one cell in a cosmic Being.

21

Turning Point in the Human Story

As the majority of humanity become filled with the finer appreciation of our individual participations in human evolution, we will open our minds and hearts to being receptive to the overall enhancement of the Divine Presence within us.

Our willingness to explore new options and practices in our personal reality is helping us to shape the evolving consensus of opinions and beliefs about the whole. In fact, our personal insights, acted upon in faith and knowing that success is certain, make it possible to alter the course upon which the main body of humanity is moving.

The universe is an integrated Being of many aspects that constitute a whole consciousness. The universe is an integrated Entity that views each of us as a cell of living power that is able to alter the whole in much the same way that the cells of a human body affect the whole body. The universe is affected by every person's indigence, illness, or wellness. The universe is a formless yet living Mind, brought into a comprehensive focus through the anticipations of all its aspects: us. The universe is a free-thinking, synergistic representative of the minds of us all.

We constitute the fabric of existence—by our demeanors, our truth, and our hope. *We* constitute the level of reality that surrounds us—by our visions, our single-mindedness, and our capacity to believe in devotion and bliss.

The universe is composed of our individual abilities to synergize with every other person's desire. The universe is the living expression of the awareness of all our Higher Selves, made up of our beliefs and values. The universe is a texturized formlessness of which we are elements, in the same way that the cells of our bodies are elements of the whole beings we are.

Humanity's unfolding consciousness is comparable to the unfolding consciousness of our individual perceptions. Therefore, to heal this world, it is instrumental and powerfully essential that we each take responsibility for healing our own soul wounds. As we do, we will heal the wounds of society and heal the wounds of the Consciousness of which *we* are the living voices.

How can we stretch our viewpoints into fresh concepts and ideas and a capacity to be innovative and to conceive new directions?

When we identify the estrangements that have separated us, and begin to dissolve these through our individual will to live in the light, we begin to remove the barriers that have blocked our spiritual demeanor in the world. We begin to unleash the potency of kindness inherent in us. Kindness unlocks the door of self-awareness toward which we are drawn.

In the era now before us, we of humanity will find ourselves opening conceptually and living empowered. Our living standard will be the measure of all our choices. Humanity is unfolding synchronistically as each one of us unfolds. Humanity is the vision each of us holds and expresses in our deepest understanding. As each one of us expands, so does the whole of the human race, exponentially. As each one of us unfolds toward the true Self, so does the whole of the human race, exponentially.

Every person is a part of that Being that is the living force. Every one of us represents the consciousness of humanity, by: our personal devotion to all that is holy, as we understand it; our personal dedication to all that is good, as we understand it; and our synchronicity with the forces of the universe.

In whatever way we comprehend it, each of us is reshaping the texture of human life.

22

Next Level of the Human Species

The Divine Mind gives us ten new Universal Laws to live by, called the "Tenets of Clear Being," so that we can be the persons we were born to be.

Tenets of Clear Being

1. *Be in the moment that you are.*

2. *Be exactly where you are.*

3. *Acknowledge your highest level of being.*

4. *Appreciate yourself.*

5. *Appreciate others.*

6. *Exude a clear presence.*

7. *Invoke a clear conscience.*

8. *Honor the highest range of affection.*

9. *Live in the beliefs of goodwill.*

10. *Give of yourself when needed.*

To register these attributes and be a fully realized human who kindles inner wisdom and appreciates daily miracles, synthesize with your complete essential Self.

By accentuating our whole being, we open our awareness to an upward spiral of increasing sensitivity. We acquire a cosmic outlook and the intellect of a seer. We fully develop our ideal Self. We synthesize with our higher Nature. We so sweetly surrender to our possible being that we embrace our inner truth with grace.

It is possible to be fully actualized while in the present body. To be more of the innate spiritual being you were born to be, wholeheartedly align with your inner Self. Embrace its eternal concepts. Form your fullness by being in sync with the natural order of life and completely in harmony. To manifest your goodness, live as your exponential Self.

Sometimes it seems the human species will never evolve. We certainly do not seem sensitive to our divine Character. Yet by nature all things do evolve. All beings become more than they were. All animals, plants, minerals, even the very atoms of the universe, continually evolve.

We of humanity are very fortunate. We are living during a time of great expansion. Humanity is destined to evolve into a greater breadth of awareness, to become a greater expression of the whole of God, to be in spiritual bodies of consciousness. It is as natural for the human race to ascend in the cosmic spectrum as it is for the amoebae to evolve.

Humanity is on the threshold of a new planetary culture, energizing self-consciousness with a higher altitude, embodying higher aspects of self-reflection. We are living during a time of unparalleled change ... and we cannot stop this concert of our uniqueness. We cannot hold back our innate power, nor delay our higher Stature. All that we are becoming is now unfolding. We are deeded this trust by the God within. Its current is transforming us.

Its breath is molding us. Its fuse of hope is inspiring us. Our inner delight is now unfolding.

To embrace this cosmic stretching, to embolden your inner light and come into the full flower of your true Self:

- Adhere to the "Tenets of Clear Being."

- Become that point of view, that attitude, that essence.

To find the confidence to go on, to hold to your dream and keep your inner flame alive:

- Surrender to the presence of the Divine Consciousness that is in you.

- Allow the Mind Force to imbue you.

- Desire its form in your body, breathe its fire of surrender, and reconstruct your body to its higher dimension by accepting the wisdom of your soul within you.

- Accentuate your soul's devotions through your feelings.

- Liberate your soul's concepts through your intellect.

- Embrace your soul's kindness through your heart.

Humanity is becoming such a people. We are all babies within a cosmic womb. The placenta is the cosmic awareness of our becoming Selves.

Humanity, the hour is upon us. In due time, we will have fully birthed. In the womb of the Eternal Mother, we are being taught. We are closely linked to that Presence that gives us life. We are infused with its consciousness, alive in its embrace.

We will never become extinct. We will not obliterate ourselves. The Eternal Selves promise that we cannot. They promise that we cannot stop the onward flow. We may resist, but we cannot stop the process of our spiritual evolution.

Today, we are investing in that future world. We are creating the state of our actualized beings, and we are well able. At last, we are moving out of our darkness, releasing our dim sight, breaking free of our old secrets and pains. We are beginning to fathom our potential and to invoke our inner truth: that we are innately good and one with the whole of creation.

As we continue on our present course, increasingly we will access our unique spiritual power. We will discipline ourselves in the arts of self-will and self-love and consciously give of ourselves to this process, because we cannot otherwise be happy with who we are.

Our central attribute as human beings is our ability to stretch. Humanity is now stretching. Soon we will be leaving the womb of the Eternal Mother. Soon we will be newborn beings of light.

Revealed Teachings

Volume II

Transcending

Part I

Humanity in Transformation

A step.
This is it.
We begin.
We are on the threshold of a new world,
embracing our greater Selves,
finishing with visions of hatred,
realizing that our sojourn is
creator-being.

Earth Mother,
you have nursed your babes.
We are restless,
ready to tear away from the comfort of known realms.
Mother, what will become of us?
How will we know?

Child,
we are here,
always you are cared for ... still.

Life breathes
and we fly.
Shall we venture out of our cocoons?
Shall we know that our agonies are dreams and our hopes
reality yet to be?

Divine essence born within leads us on,
we,
angels kin.
Earth is breaking anew
and, we,
sojourners of restored Identities.

Journeys of life are endless.
Gods walked with us when first we came to be.
We knew the elements.
We lived in peace.

Now we experiment with divine compassion
and tread higher thought
— reconnecting and remembering.

The cosmos is our being,
keeping us in its love,
and we, just now, are opening ourselves.
We have been blind.

The cosmos is our parent.
"Yet even I," says the unborn seed, "am God."
And so now we birth,
and pause to consider,
we are transcending.

The only pain is our umbilical boundaries
of mind and heart.
Until we tear away from the safety of our known realities
and spread our light into the skies of our esteem,
will we be brave enough to believe in who we are
... and be it?

We came here from the stars.
Earth,
home,
is a stop along the way in our travels from early essence.

Earth Mother,
beloved being,
we now break free from our wombs of indecision.
We leap into our higher will,
blessed.

With the Presence as our counselor,
we are devotees
of our god
our unlimited Selves.
Can we walk boldly and *be*?

Carried no more.
Our Brethren who spoke throughout many lives on Earth
now let us go.
Not for lack of love
but for our own steps into a new cosmic understanding.

Like children
leaving the womb of darkness
crying our first cries of ecstasy,
we are coming into a brighter
more exultant reality —
what we were born to be.

Crescendo of Possibilities

Feel the illumination of this hour, for life is now taking a leap into its full breadth. Life is expanding its reach. Bursting forth.

We are threading the impossible. And now a new form of integrity is critically reaching a crescendo. We are now ready to release our hidden terrors.

We are embarking upon an industrious new vista and a new capacity to conceive solutions. An undercurrent of wisdom is now breaking through our old reasonings.

We have seen hardship and now we are steadfast leaders of making right the balance. We are solvers. We are those leading the fearful out of their haunted lives.

We are not the deceit of past threats, by us or to us. We are not the anguish of what has hurt us, nor the burdens of what has limited us. We are not what haunts us. We are what emboldens us. We are leaders with the vision to go a new way.

Life is at hand. New treatments, science, and technology. All are now reaching a crescendo of possibility. Humanity has entered a new threshold, and there is no going back.

The old ways will fade. In time, they will be history. Life as we have known it is transcending. We can stay in the old, or we can embrace the vision that inspires us.

Why are we alive, *now?* To kindle our vision so that its breadth overlights the whole. To share the dream that inspires us.

Every transition in human expansion has come with resistance. But come it will. And our dreams, realized, are the fodder of *the new humanity.*

A New World Is Dawning

Life is the moments we are awake in our full Self. The moments when we lift others up.

At this time, the entire human species is transcending (*The Transcension*) into the next dimension of self-awareness. This is felt as *expanded insight.* Our ability to *visualize* new ideas and to be aware of *all* as a single body of life is transcending.

As we individually transcend, new *insights* are born within us and new visions are now within our reach.

This does not mean all of our problems go away. We must still act with reason and courtesy. We must still act without bias or judgment. We still have to learn how to be our ideal Selves.

What *is* changing is our ability to see and sense what once was a mystery. More is now within the reach of our higher Imagination, wherein lie the answers to what perplexes us and the secrets to life. Less is unknowable.

Thus, now as all the world is shifting, let us Imagine life the way we want it.

It is first *Ideas* from which come inspirations and intuitions. > *Thought* is the precursor to reality manifest. > *Imagination* is the precursor to thoughts directed.

So, live with hope and allow the forces of life to Create through you. That is when you know you are an evolving human. That is when you know *you* are embracing the fullness to which you were born.

Explosion of Awareness

Humanity is in an explosion of *awareness,* the path to understanding our oneness with God and with each other.

We are *still* in evolution: Our body, but also our insatiable drive to learn, to know more, to give, to help, and to create. We are *now* evolving into a new level of what it means to be human. We are becoming more.

December 22, 2012 was a doorway. The inner Counselor is our lamp and shows us our wisdom and our strength.

All that we need do is *listen.*

Social Tsunami

There is now a wave of personal enforcement crossing the world like a tsunami. A passionate social expansion.

The lands of old ideas have been like a cave of dark shadows. Now arising is a force of goodness that cannot and will not be forestalled. In all lands that have for millennia been encumbered in ideologies of power and rule, now arising is a force of such presence that it shakes loose the very foundations of dead dreams and those in power who would choose harm over goodwill. In those lands that have seen their own shadows, where only the leaders have prospered, now arising is a vigor and an indomitable and charismatic force of expansion for *all* peoples.

These changes have been foreseen. It is *now.* This is a new day.

The effects are multitudinous. Not one nation can hide from its responsibility. Not one nation can ignore the destructive powers outside its borders. For what happens in one place, happens in another.

The world has become a single city. What happens outside our "walls" does affect our lives in every substantial way. When we stand on moral right—for *all* peoples—we are standing for a world in which we can feel not only safe but invigorated and renewed.

Today is a day to be glad. We are in a trend toward necessary restoration of what all peoples seek:

To live without fear of our life and safety. To live with hope. To live with a heart at peace.

The Counterweight of Power

The world is stressed under great alterations in belief systems. Old beliefs are crumbling.

Destiny is now upon us. New insights are taking root.

Individual value is based on insight, courage, and fortitude; not on power. Power is nothing without its *counterweight:* caring.

We are now in a time of total change. How can you know what to do?

Listen. Let your inner knowing be the only voice that leads you. Heed not those who rant, nor those who challenge actions done in goodwill. Heed only the inner counsel of reason, which is found in the inner quiet, wherein we learn how to live humbly, simply and honorably, respecting all.

Floodlight Through the World

The cries for freedom are a floodlight in all the world and will not—will not—be restrained. Wherever peoples are being shut down, shut up, shut in—the forces that dominate will crumble, are crumbling, from within. Those who do not heed eventually will be unable to withstand the bright fortitude of the Many.

Today is a new day.

Even in a particularly dark corner of the earth, where millions have lived downtrodden on bare subsistence, generation after generation after generation, there is a splinter, from within. This

Kingdom, unknown by most, not understood by the multitudes, already has begun to crack, from within.

This is a day to put forth support of all hearts, in all lands, who are seeking the right to hold up their heads, both women and men, to show their faces and shine their truth.

This is a day to strengthen our commitment to help all who are dying to help their people. To stand for the many. For today, the many are ready. The many will not, any longer, cower. Their hearts speak, "We want to be free!"

These are not simple days. But these are the days long foretold. And it is now.

Conscience Is the New Humanity

There are no more shadows within which to crouch. The Light is sweeping out all old disdain and the false illusions of what strength is. All the world is shifting. Awakening. Conscience is born.

Conscience is *the new humanity.*

Conscience is the essence of our true Self. It is us stripped of savagery. It is us stripped of gloating and fear, which are only an empty sense of personal worth.

Conscience is the voice of our true Self. When we heed our conscience, our life unfolds in gratitude, and generosity pours itself upon us.

When we ignore our conscience, we lose contentment.

Contentment is the opposite of reckless seeking, and is the result of living with respect for all living things. When we live with respect, life honors us and we are blessed.

The Transcension

Life is brimming with possibility and opportunities are flowing continuously all around us. We can now absorb ingenuity, using

Reasoned Perception. This is when we activate our brain's electrodes, which are the source of creative expression and the necessary component for lifting our veil of confusion.

When we are *activated,* our brain's neuro paths organize and reorganize into *new* sensory receptiveness. We become aware of life's extraordinary colors and spectrums. We feel the full breadth of ideas and thoughts. We can imagine the unimaginable— because we have opened a *new* brain center.

This is the "awakening of the whole" and is the beginning of a continued opening. Like the petals of a flower, we blossom, one petal at a time.[3]

This evolutionary awareness is called a *spiritual awakening.* In actuality, our brain is being rewired. The neuro pathways are changing. Areas of the brain that, before, were dormant are now "waking up."

While this "awakening" *feels* spiritual, actually our entire being is altering. Our depth of perception is becoming far lighter and we are now on the path of the "full embodiment of our wholeness."

This is why we are taught to be still, to feel, to listen, to breathe. This is also why and how our lives can transform. Because once our brain and body "arrive" into a more fused state of the Light (that we are), all else becomes more and more merely an extension of our imagination.

Once we are fused into our Light Essence, which then begins to function as a *beacon,* then what we imagine is more exactly as we have envisioned it. Our ability to bring into life the beauty our heart seeks now feels almost miraculous.

So breathe and be glad. We are already, or are near, this "awakening to my Presence."

So also is the breadth of the human race. This is the step that all of humanity, one at a time, are now undergoing— *The Transcension.*[4]

---

3 For more on this topic, read *The Soul Path.*

4 For more on this topic, read *The New Humans* (book 2 "The New Humanity" series).

Amplified Intuition

It is in our capacity to perceive circumstances that intend danger, to know what surrounds us in any situation, to *feel* and intuit other people's thoughts and emotions.

We are now beginning to reach toward a more enlightened perspective on the abilities of being human, to stretch toward amplifying our innate intuitive abilities. This is now activating in everyone.

Those born since 1975 are already aware. Others are now being awakened, intrinsically, to this inherent tendency to know what is *about* to occur. To *sense* it.

All events are in constant movement and are discernable. All we need do is be aware. It's a *subtle* sense: a prickly feeling, a sudden knowing, the hair standing on your arms, your back tingling, or a sudden intense inexplicable rush (such as a sudden fear or worry that strikes you, i.e. premonition).

We already know these senses. *Now* they are enhancing.

When we give focus to our sensibilities, we prevent harm and avoid what is about to occur. We can perceive an imminent threat— that is not yet evident consciously but will occur in a fraction of a second, enough time to stop in our tracks and avoid the incident.

Forewarned is safety.[5]

Expanded Perceptions

A tremendous surge of brain neurons is rewiring the human brain, in all born since 2001. This is the generation of expanded perceptions, heightened capacity, and enlarged occipital lobe.

These are the future of human beings. They have more complex nervous systems and a greater ability to comprehend. They have an innate ability to view the whole, not just the parts. They have an

---

5 For examples of how this all works, read my workbook *Intuition for Every Day*.

inner-senses system that allows them to know truth from lie—and to seek truth and ignore lie. They also are adept at discerning falsehoods in all forms, and will decry (call out) anyone who intentionally distorts the basic fundamental goodness of human nature.

These new minds are the highest of any ever born before on Earth. They are the wisest in heart. They see and feel the pain of the animal kingdom, the cruelty of murderers and torturers. They decry, vigilantly, all who harm any others. Especially, they stand up to all who harm children, who mislead children, who abuse children. For these new minds have a heightened sensibility of value and honesty, fairness and judgment. They do not tolerate deceivers. They will, in fact, rise up against them.

These bright minds, born since 2001, are the light in the dark storm of confusion. They see clearly. They speak abruptly. They act boldly.

These are the first generation of Humanity 2.0.

Unlike others who have gone before them, they adapt quickly, they learn swiftly, and they grasp life's conundrums with the wisdom of sages. They must. For such insight is needed, now.

They bring forth the answers to earth's problems: the pollution, the scars, the disruptions to earth's natural balance. These bright minds disregard fools. They are intent on restoring balance. They are the keepers of the earth and, more than any before them, they understand the balance of nature and its essential intersection with human life.

They are born, now, to restore earth's balance and humanity's heart. Humanity is prone to self-absorption. These new bright minds are sages, bringing order in the midst of all who disrupt. They restore the order of the natural world. After which, the rest of humanity are able to stop their madness, to pause, take a breath and regroup.

The salvation of the human species, prone to self-absorption, is those who now stand up and say:

"No more. You are destroying this world, and it stops now. We are here to heal this world. Let us lead you. We hear the earth. We feel the sorrow. We decry the selfish aggrandizers. No longer will one's kingship be allowed to destroy others. Those days are over. We are here to bring order, and to heal the wounds of the earth.

"We are here to heal the wounds of the children as well. Watch out. Cruelty is no longer an option and will no longer be tolerated. We are the watchers. We are here to restore goodwill. We live only to bring back the senses of the group. Humanity thrives only as a whole. We are here to restore the whole."

Why Are Any of Us in Life?

We are in life to be our whole being, not the few ideas of our culture. We are more than our limitations, more than the misconceptions of the world, more than a faceless nameless self who seems to be lost in the human masses.

We each have a fire of insight, a gift of resonance, and a talent for illuminating. We each have a full grasp of *all that is.* We are each a realist and also an idealist ... who *knows* we are part of a whole.

We know, at our core, that we are part of a Greater Self. We have an inner sense of *all that is.* We know that the Divine Will lives *through* us, that life is not to be carelessly denied; that life is the vision deep in us and is why we are here, and that our insights are not only for us, they are *our* connection to the whole.

Becoming

We are not our body; our body is an extension of us. We are not our brain; our brain is the tool through which we are able to function.

What are we? We are Life Force, the innate element considered to be Thought > which is the element considered to be Idea > which is the element considered to be Imagination > which *is* Consciousness. We are not our body. We are consciousness.

Why does it help to know this? Because consciousness is *how* we create, how we manifest, how we draw events to us—through our ability to conceptualize *beyond* what we have been taught.

With an actively directed Consciousness, we can *cause* circumstances to enhance our deepest needs. With an actively charged conscious vibration in and *through* our brain and body, we can *feel* the changes taking place.

When Conscious, we feel *all that is* and our place in it. And we can bring to ourselves what we need to be happy and safe, to survive and to build.

We are not our body. We are our Mind. And our mind is not our brain. Our mind is *all that is*.[6]

We all are a part of a vast Ocean of Mind. In this way, we can know: all that is occurring, in the moment and in the moments before us.

Nothing is contained. Everything is accessible.

What we believe is limited is not limited. What we believe is concrete is not concrete.

Substance is not life. Water is not life. These are merely forms through which *life* becomes physical. The nature of all life, in all existence, all dimensions, all realities, is consciousness.

Life *is* consciousness.

---

6 For more on this discussion, read my Appendix "Holism: A New Trend in Humanity's Consciousness," a UCCS philosophy paper I wrote in 1985-87.

Consciousness is the source of everything that is. It cannot be bound. It cannot be repressed. It cannot be constrained.

Consciousness is Eternal Being. It is the source of *all that is.* It is the very nature of worlds and all upon them. It is the composition. What we call life is an *extension* of Consciousness.

As Consciousness, humanity we are transcending. One by one, we are changing: in our thoughts, in our capacity to Reason, in our ability to Dream. We are *now* becoming.

Coded In Us

It may look as if all things are solid. They are not. It may look as if our body is "wired" to age. It is not. This is an effect of encoding.

Our physical world is the effect of our understanding the mutable state of all living forms: earth, seas, plant life, animal life, higher-conscious humans and animals (such as whales and dolphins).

Nothing is immutable. All things are infinite, in degrees. Physical reality is also altering. It is malleable, not fixed. It is resonant to other levels of being, not finite.

Earth is transcending and life on Earth is transcending.

Layers of reality co-exist. Life co-exists simultaneously in layers. Reality is *multi-dimensional.* So that, all worlds are *at-one* in time, and uplifting their frequencies to a new *layer* of "reality."

Now, what has been the "norm" is no longer the *final* function. Third dimension is finite; fourth dimension is not. And *now* Earth and all on it are transcending vibrationally into the fourth-dimension physical.

This *new* earth is a vibrational development unlike humans have known before. This new earth looks the same. It isn't. It is a new world of a new kind of human: aware.

Not only is the earth transcending vibrationally, humanity is also lifting in resonance. We are transcending—in genetic makeup: awakening our layers of *encoding* to a higher creativity.

This is the *new human, the new humanity.*

The new human knows. Nothing is hidden. You see all.

You are now beginning to digest this, beginning to comprehend it, because you are now beginning to feel the *real* world, with senses that are vivid and expanded, senses that grasp the continuity of all life, senses that think *beyond* the body.

You are now awaking to a new *layer* of physical reality. That new layer is now activated. It is now visible. You see it. You already live it.

You may be aware of insights that seem to come on their own, ideas that just arrive, sensibilities that blow away beliefs you were taught.

You may find yourself knowing what someone is feeling, thinking, about to do. Then they do it. These "traits" have been hidden. Now they are awake. You are awake.

With this also comes a deeper understanding of your spiritual responsibility. With this also comes grace.

The new human is mature, not childish. The new human is wise, not insensitive. The new human forgives, does not run away.

You are a new human. That is why you are here.

Earth Next

Today's illuminated concepts about the universe and matter already have opened a window into alternate layers of solid worlds.

We live simultaneously in layers of parallel vibratory frequencies. Some of this is known now, already, in the scientific global community. This new understanding, beyond *all* previous studies and accepted norms, is a window into truly beginning to grasp the nature of universes and energy—which is the *source* of all.

Energy is the essential *element* of all life. It is not physical in origin; physicality is only an apparent feature. More aptly, energy is Thought. Energy is the stuff of life and *all* matter. Energy is the Original Forces.

Understanding that energy comprises everything *is* the new, now opened, window that will elevate (and propel) humanity from our past—into a new era of constructive developments all over the earth: to organize, build, develop, and create; with a new higher vibratory perceptual ability to operate together for a higher good. Humanity will, and can, alter our dominant behavior pattern of self-destruction.

As a species, we already have crossed a threshold. Now before us is a completely new *layer* of existence—a new layer (level) of physical life. Now before us is not merely choosing control or dominance over others; that is the past, which *will* subside, like a tide going out.

Now before us, available to us, is a new ability: to envision options that were not previously known, to grasp better choices than ever dreamed; more importantly, to engineer the structures that comprise it and design it. Now, today, work comes in the ability to design new forms of directing *energy* in all its forms, animate and inanimate.

This earth and all upon it are alive. Life is changing, in *layers.* Human beings' old layer (level of conscious being) was destruction, cruelty, self-absorption, and judgment.

The new *layer* of human reality—Earth and beyond, Earth Next, *Earth Nexus*—has arrived. We are *now* experiencing *The Transcension* (transformation) from the old dense third vibration into the fourth level (dimension) of physical life. We are pulling and stretching. Feel it? *The future is now.* We have entered **Earth Nexus.**

We already sense it. We feel it.

It is a better life. But it does require opening our inner vision and the ability to perceive and comprehend nuances. It does require inviting growth (rather than hiding from it or resisting it).

Not everyone is able to understand. Many are afraid and resist. With them, we must be patient. (June 12, 2011)

Cosmos Evolving

Life did not just happen once. It is always arising. This is the basic model: Imagine, construct, observe, allow, generate, flourish ... and again, over and over, infinitum.

There is not a finite limit to anything. Life is not bound by Earth's construction. Life *is* evolution and is *always* being generated.

Our world is in this state also. To understand this, observe the natural ebb and flow of all around you. Nature.

What is burgeoning forth now—a lighter vibrational frequency— does so *through* the existing form, which then falls away, making room for the new.

Life is only now truly beginning to expand as a vibrant, energetic force that is dynamic, exquisite, and unbound. All that we have observed, thus far, about our world—its grandeur, its splendor—imagine it exponentially even more resonant, more vivid. Imagine our evolving world as also "waking up," only now truly becoming the extraordinary place it is meant to be.

The *Deep Thought* is continuously developing new vacuums through which it manifests new life forms. It is in these vacuums that life arises. The *Deep Mind* is an *Energy Consciousness* that continuously evokes the creative evolutionary spark, which is eternal and ever developing.

Now, also visualize humanity evolving in this same way, to: more insightful, with a deeper reverence for all life and a deeper comprehension of our inherent divine nature.

The new is burgeoning forth *through* the old, which will fall away. This is also what is happening to us. Something new is burgeoning from deep within us, awakening in us an exquisite sensibility.

It is as if for the first time, we are truly awake.

Humanity Not an Accident
Greenhouse Earth

Life is not an accident. Humanity is not an accident. Earth life is a planned evolution of species; one greenhouse, within which, overtime, multiple kinds of species originate.

To grasp the Concepts beyond what is known, we must release our walls of preconceptions. Earth's nature, humanity's nature, and the nature of the cosmos are such preconceptions. Once we open our Idea process, we are on the verge of truly awakening to the nature of life beyond what we already have perceived.

Our world is an ongoing greenhouse, in which multiple forms of life exist; some we know, some we do not, some are still in the phase of "generation" (pre-manifestation) and will be but are not yet.

Life is ongoing, regardless of the state of conditions. There are many forms of organisms. Not all are human, and not all are composed of the same ingredients. Life merely means "aware of itself."

Earth's body is not unique, yet it is a familiar type of system in which life forms function. In the *millenniums* ahead, humanity (as others before us) will learn how to find these earths.

This century and the next we will be learning how to heal our suffering, both mental and physical. As we evolve as a species, we will think more clearly and care more deeply. We will be less angry and more willing to listen. We will be less afraid and more willing to be content.

We Came from Other Worlds

Human DNA is comparable to alien DNA. We are from other worlds.

Humans did not begin on Earth. Earth is not our first home.

We came into lands already filled with all animals of all species. Whales in great abundance, as in its beginning this world was mostly seas and oceans. The land rose slowly over many thousands of years.

As the first of our species, human, we had travelled far. From the Pleiades first. Then Orion and Sirius. Then other star systems.

Humans have been since the start of physical reality. We have, therefore, evolved into many states of body, then many levels of consciousness (energy mind).

When we were first on Earth, we were in an early stage of these developments. We did not arrive fully developed. We needed to accommodate to the environment, which was active and volatile. So we started here in the form called Homo Sapiens, an unevolved human being but suited to the land.

Now the human species is in the phase called *Transcension,* during which we quickly evolve.

Actually, we did go through an evolutionary spurt once before: the Renaissance, when our capacity to imagine took hold.

Now we are in our *second* growth spurt, when the capacity to imagine is crucial.

So, we are evolving. It begins with dormant intelligence sparking and activating within the individual.

You know if you are there. You *feel* it. How do you get there?

- *Intention* to live as the best person you can be.

- *An open mind.* Always learning, stretching, and not accepting defeat, for there is always an answer, always a solution.

- *An open heart.* Willing to be kind, tolerant, and forgiving, which creates peace of mind.

- *Courage and resolve*—to live and act as your inner knowing guides and drives you.

- *Expanding* your creative expressions, following your dream.

- *Listening* to the still small inner Counselor that is always present to offer ideas and insights.

- *Meditating,* daily—in order to breathe in the Presence of the Divine, into your mind and body.

These are what teach us and develop us.

When we do these things, daily, with thoughtfulness, we evolve. It simply comes.

We are evolving consciousness, which affects the evolution of our brain and body.

Consciousness comes first. It is always there.

Now, this lifetime, we have a choice: Muddle through, or strive. Will we be all that we can be? It is in us to expand.

You, now, already have all the talents you need to *be* your best Self.

Living from the Awareness lifts us up. And the time is now.

Heart Truth

This century, this millennium, humanity is *officially* universal.

Yes, we are still coming into knowledge. Yes, we are still reaping the results of past deeds. Yes, we are still searching for the meaning of life.

Yet we are in a new state of human existence. We are past the threshold. We are through the doorway.

What our heart believes is what will be, for *all* of us, for *each* of us.

Part II

You the Bringer of Light

You Are a Bringer of Light

The lives that others lead have nothing to do with how you feel the *living divine* through you. No other is you.

Listen to your own inner counsel. Therein is the resonant serenity. Only in the pure inner stillness is there any real understanding—for it is the house of divine wisdom.

To release uncertainty, anger, judgment, and sadness—find the stillness within. There is your pure being. There you *know* who you truly are.

You, dear one who is reading this, you are a bringer of Light, for all whose lives you see, feel, and know. You are with the angels, by your truthful and caring inner-core strength. You are a carrier of Light—and the world hungers for Light.

Hold your Light out. Be the Light you know is within you. Let your own spiritual center be the presence that leads you. It is you, dear one. It is you.

Light is an open heart, a nature of gratitude, a presence of humility, a service of compassion. Be the Light that is already in you. In this way, you are graced with serenity.

You Are the Conductor of Your Life's Rhythms

Life is your Mind dreaming, imagining. What do you want? Create it—through your hopes > which generate ideas > which optimize possibilities.

You are the conductor of the ebb and flow in your life. Be aware of the projections and you can direct the opportunities. Be aware of your inevitable role and you attract goodwill.

The secret to contentment is to live for bringing hope into others' lives. Share your ideas and you are creating a constancy of new consequences, which unfold in your life like the ebb and flow of the earth's seas.

Feel the pulse of life's rhythms. Therein is the sensitivity to awakening to the wholeness of all life.

When we are in life's rhythm and it is in us, our moments effortlessly move us to where we need to be.

Find your inner place, the *stillpoint* amidst life's ripples, and *you* are in life's true harmony.

Stillness, As the World Rumbles in Chaos

You, my friend, are a bringer of stability in the midst of chaos.

Your willingness to hold a vigil to lift others up is the crucial moment toward a deeper spiritual awareness, for *truth* is found in surrender to the peaceful *presence* within.

The personal reservoir of *presence* is who you are in your sweet comforting of those who are troubled and desperate. You are a reservoir of relief to those who need hope. Be the *presence* you feel is inside you. Therein, even when troubled, you are able to be at peace.

No matter how things seem, no matter how much the world's noise is like a rumble letting loose across the airwaves, no matter how much the cries and desperation of millions are like a throttling of all hope, humanity, we are in a new life, struggling to find a new sense of Purpose. This is a new awareness piercing the density of the compelling dissonance. This is a new life threading through the very breath of all the confounding voices.

Despite the surface chaos, despite the unparalleled and resounding shattering noise, inside you is a penetrating quiet. Deep inside you, stillness.

Be still ... and breathe.

In stillness is your peace. Clarity follows.

For now ... just be.

The Universal Hum Resonating Through You

Have faith in your ability to be wise. Know that you are already adapted to insight and capacity. You already have the heart ability to live in a state of clear mental awareness.

Thinking *in* hope, thinking *in* imagination—*these* open you to the inner *presence* and your Mind's endless capacity. Your Mind is able to reach beyond your surroundings. Your Mind is not bound to your brain. Your Mind is part of a Collective and, in that, you can *breathe into* a visionary capacity—to *feel,* sense, and empathically reach out to *all that is* (and ever will be).

Your abilities as a human are not limited to being physical. Your Thoughts can open you up, in the *heart-breath,* to the scope of the greater life—of which you are a part. You today, now, already can access this. It is in, and through, the deep inner being you are.

Your body is a tool. Your Mind is a tool. Your True Potential is in your access of the inner You. This Self you are is always present, always in you; always sensitive, open, and giving.

This is the Self you *feel* in your moments of Insight and revelation. This is the Self you sense when Awareness strikes, like a resonance, a *note* of absolute understanding. In that Resonance, you have a deeply *felt connection* to something extraordinary. That something is the true You. It's who you really are.

How grand is the whole You. How limitless. You feel fully alive. Fully tapped in. Fully embraced by such a deep Resonance, at your core, that you get it. You simply know.

Sometimes it is not explained in words, this Deepness that resonates through you like a rhythm, so intangible yet so vital, awakening you to the greatness you sense is in you.

No matter where you are, no matter the deepest hatreds against you, no matter the harsh tragedies wrought upon you (or that you have wrought upon others), *you* have this inner Self softly humming inside you, always there, gently nudging.

Feel it, *sense* it, the inner knowing that angels are always with you, speaking in your heart: *We are here.*

Yes, you must choose. Yes, it is your gift to go out into the world and be an example. Yes, it is your responsibility to use your higher attitude to *resonate* in the world in a way that *in* you is like a chime softly ringing, echoing. This inner resonance changes who you are *into* the Fullness for which you yearn. It is in you, now. [7]

> *Feel* it... Be still... *Breathe...*
>
> Breathe...... Slow down....... Slow down..................
>
> Feel the deep, long, soft, easy, universal *hum* in and *through* you—as you are part of it. You are one in it.
>
> This universal hum is Life. It is your breath. It is *you* in rhythm with the essence of *all that is...*
>
> Now be still and breathe... deeply... gently... into the inner calm............

---

[7] For more exercises like this, study my workbook *Intuition for Every Day.*

Remembering and Reconnecting to Your Pure Original Self

Life's troubles are not a punishment, reprisal, or judgment. It is the nature of human existence.

The concept of suffering has, for all of human history, made humans feel insignificant—as if we are manipulated and controlled by forces outside of us. This has led to false beliefs and escaping personal responsibility.

No outer Being judges our actions. Rather, in the difficult events, we are seeing:

- The nature of humans in our state of confusion and forgotten heritage.

- The physical dimensions, which function by physical laws, the scope still to be understood.

- The innate Presence of the beings known as angels, who are a distinct species.[8]

- The innate divinity of humans, whose origin is the Divine Realm.

What does this mean?

- We get to choose our feelings, our thoughts, our responsibilities, our behaviors.

- We get to believe whatever helps us to be thoughtful to others.

---

8 For more on who and what are angels, read *Wings of Light* and *Walking with Angels* (2018).

- We get to recognize the self-*centered*ness of our Original Self, who *is* attuned to life and does sense and feel a relationship to the whole of life (all peoples, all cultures, the animals, the earth).

- We get to identify and act upon the talents in our personality as an avenue to creatively give to others.

This life, while filled with difficulties that are often incomprehensible, is an opportunity to lift ourselves up into a demeanor that is kind, thoughtful, patient, and longsuffering.

Yes, this is usually felt in a single moment's awareness. Yes, these moments are often out of sync with our actions. Yes, we fail, often, in our ability to be wise and tolerant.

Yet this is both the gift and the hardship of human life. For when we are able to focus our moments in the heart and find the grace that *is* there, in those moments we know, humbly, *"I am."*

It is the nature of human life to polarize, to challenge. This forces us to be aware, to feel. If we do not feel, if we do not hurt, we cannot know how to lift others up.

We are in this life to: Heal our soul wounds. Heal others' soul wounds. Heal the earth's wounds.

All living things are conscious, in their own way. Humans have the sacred honor to remember, humbly, *"I am."*

We are from the Divine Realm, born in the Essential Self, pure. We are our Essential Self, now. Each moment, returning to our Natural State, relearning, remembering.

Life is the place to learn: how to heal our anger, how to forgive others' unawareness, how to allow differences.

It is not by chance that humans are all so distinct. This is life. *All* living things are Selves, with individual insights, perceptions, skills, and needs. Even the animals. Even the angels are unique. None is like any other.

Mainly, know this: No Being judges us. All beings are unique, even angels.

You are an Essential Self whose origin is the Divine Realm. You are, now, reinstating a deeper oneness with your own True Nature.

You are now exploring who you really are. Through this journey, you are one of four billion who is resonating to a new frequency of feeling—which is the heart.

All you need to know each day is, is your heart happy? Are you at peace? If yes, breathe in gratitude and continue your service. If no, pause, listen, allow ... regroup ... and breathe.

Breathe in the healing. It is there, now. It is already in you.

Our Light Is a Beacon

The wisdom and clarity of the inner Counselor is the Divine touching our hearts, the calming presence of the Divine pervading us, the calming presence that stirs our hope and moves us to seek, humbly, that which belongs to all.

We are in a time of choice, a time to know who we are: all God's children.

Yes, there are changes. Yes, many trials. *But know this:* We are each a beacon, and we are embarking on a life that will, in time, be the ideal.

It is our nature to be a Light, and Light that will not be quenched and will not be contained.

Our hearts are pushing us toward *living* our dreams.

Travails Teach Compassion

The travails of life are opportunities to care: for those whose lives are altered, those who fear, those who have no insight beyond their deep depression.

This is our opportunity to lift up others and ourselves.

This is our new life: To live *our* destiny. To raise the Light of personal choice for all. To instill courage and faith, and embolden the mothers and fathers who distress. It is our voices that define the days before us.

Dear friends, *we* are a new life force on Planet Earth, bringing our heartfelt courage to bear upon those who harbor tortuous control.

This is our time. Our actions determine the fate of all the earth: choosing compassion and personal rights, or adhering to the ideologies long past that have controlled everyone's fates and daily lives.

This is a time to comfort those who sorrow, to help those who need someone to hear, to care, and to make time for those who seek our wisdom.

This is a new day, to live our own hearts' dreams.

Our Shining Lights

Courage and commitment are a bright force that illuminates everyone.

We are examples to others around us. Our faith, our constancy, amidst our own troubles, help others to feel assured and calm.

We are in a time of great challenge, it is true. Thus, this is a time to be wise and to be *aware.*

Our life is our *heart* and how we respect those around us. Our life is how we lift others up.

The measure of our lives is not what happens to us. It is how we share what we have learned. The measure of our lives is not the suffering thrown against us. It is our innate and amazing presence through all that comes upon us.

We are voices for others in their pain. In that comes their calm and their solutions.

The Healing Force of Human Suffering

When our heart is free of hatred, we are in our Fullness. When our mind is free of weakness and obsession, we are in our essential Nature. When our thoughts are conscious of our frailties, we are awake to our own attributes so that we will not torment ourselves.

Knowing who we are is the key to humility, wherein we are able to tap our higher Self (which is always with us).

Our higher Self is that wholeness we feel when our sole intent is to bring good into others' lives. In this state, we recognize our reverence and gentle strength, and we are filled with gratitude—which is the healing force of human suffering. Gratitude heals us.

In gratitude, we surrender our judgment, of others and ourselves. In gratitude, we forget our anguish and we value the good in others and their efforts. We seal our hardships so that they fade from affecting our actions. We are in kindness, which helps us to remain poised and becomes our more continuous attribute. When in gratitude, we are able to change our reflections. Gratitude heals us.

When we are able to release judgment, anger, doubt and fear, we are in our higher Self and we are living with an open heart, in reverence—and it feels good!

The year 2011 was the onset of our higher Selves, the critical mass into feeling the higher Presence, the sensibilities of higher Vision, and the capacity to find reason where once discord and indifference reigned.

The year 2011 was *The Transformation* of all we had believed was fundamentally true about humans and our world; the year when we began to see that *all* existence comes from an Eternal Source.

Dream It

The old attitudes hold us down. Now contemplate how you can restore the harmony in your own deep self.

Now is the time to develop a wider perspective about our aptitudes. Together, we can envision an organization that feeds the heart, the body, the mind, and the inner self. We can build the groups we have imagined. We can build the world we have envisioned.

If you dream it, it is yours.
If you imagine it, the next step is reality.

We are in a period of stretching—new dimensions in analysis, in comprehension. *Are* there any limits? No. There are no limits.

How can we create the answer for what ails millions? From the inner reasoning, the soul wisdom.

Life is about responsibility. There is no easy way. If you see a need, fill it. If you hurt for another, fix it. If you care for the troubled, it is yours, humbly, to address.

When we choose from a pure heart to heal a wound in society, the world is further healed.

The common good is the goal of *the new humanity.* The understanding that is expanding in every human heart is to live for the higher good.

Yes, we must take care of ourselves, our families, our loved ones. We also must take responsibility for our affect upon others. There comes a time when we must live for more than ourselves.

The Rule of Truth

The rule of truth: Be kind.

When we are not kind, we are shown the results of our mistaken behaviors. For *peace* in our own lives, our *essence* must be in peace. For *acceptance* in our own lives, our essence must be accepting. For our own lives to be favorable, our own essence must give *favor.*

These qualities are our essence when we are steeped in trust of the tides of life. These qualities are the essence of surrendering to the wise counsel of our inner being. These qualities are our essence when we let go of fear.

How do we get there? We find insight, a kind heart, and a tranquil composure in our inner quiet.

When we are able to be at ease, life is our greatest ally. Expect favor, and we have it. Expect gentle people, and they arrive. Expect understanding, and it is awakened in us. Life is what we believe.

Believe that people are caring, and caring people surround us. Believe that people are fair, and fairness is the standard given to us. Believe that we are capable, and we are. Believe that we have insight, and the Light comes on inside us.

We make our own experiences—by how we believe.

How to Access Your Full Greater Mind

Feel the Light sweeping through all humanity, healing, bringing knowledge and the understanding of personal empowerment.

Life is altering, now, at the cellular level, forever. All life. From this day forward, reason exponentially is more. Thoughts are more. Inventions are more. The Mind is now greater, larger.

Humanity *is* on the cusp of an entirely new evolutionary level of being. Never before have humans attained, nor were able to, *reason* with the Mind of Full Awareness. It is here now. You are able, now.

The way? Not through fear. The way to open the Mind, to expand higher Imagination (the ability to "think" beyond what is experienced) is through:

Letting go of self-judgment, letting go of hating all that goes against what we use to feel safe (ideas, beliefs, structures, people), letting go of feeling wholly inadequate, letting go of feeling superior.

Take a deep breath... Again... Again... Again...

Now stop.

Stop trying to figure it out. That is not how Ideas are born. They do not come from being intellectual.

Breathe. Let go. Relax into a slow deep inner well of calming *release*... Feel grace and humility and gratitude washing through you... Ah.........

Ideas come from where? The *stillness.*

Why and how is that the way to the Mind? Because, then, we let go of our extraneous thoughts, needs, wishes, desires, and fears. We are In The Moment of the Full Self.

Ah...there you are. *"There I am."*

Only in this inner space do we move into the Higher Mind (*which we are within, it's already there, around us*). The Greater Mind is the All. We are *within* it.

It is in this inner space that we have the epiphanies, the illuminations, the revelations. It is in this inner space that we connect with All. It is in this inner space that *our* unique talents expand exponentially to a greater capacity than we ever thought possible. Because the Greater Mind is limitless.

This frees us, activates us. All we have hoped for or considered, now the pieces show up for us and we begin to *see* how they fit together.

You have a unique way of learning *and* applying. In *you,* through *you,* are the solutions to humanity's perplexities.

How can you know what to contribute? Your talent? You know. You feel it. It drives you. It *speaks* to you, constantly.

Turn your full attention to the heart-welling vision that is calling to you now. Trust yourself.

The answer is: Of course it is yours to do. You dreamed it. Now make it real.

How to Direct Your Energy to Alter the World

All the changes around the earth are a part of the awareness shifting in all of humanity. Every nuanced energy is continuously rippling outward—to and through *all.*

As we Think from our center of compassion and the powerful force vibration of kindness, so expands that vibration to all around us. We each are a *part* of the world.

Our energy (abilities, time given; or meanness, self-deprecation, deprecation of others) generates a vibration outward from us. These energy ripples are *always* in flux, in a constant state of expansion, in a forever state of *creating.*

We can, with intention, enhance our daily vibration to serenity (at least at our essence).

How do you do this? And how can you know if it's working?

Sit inwardly in a state of *reverence* for all that lives.

Sit inwardly in a state of *gratitude* for all you value, in this fully enveloping moment of deep grace.

It takes only a *moment.*

When in our depth, we resonate to the pure gift of *appreciation.* It is this that heals our deep uncertainties and lightens our burdens, until hope fills us.

As hope fills us, like an eternal well, our faith is restored, in our self and life in general.

As you heal and your hope grows, your desires change from *me me me* to *"How can I serve?"*

This attitude shift turns your life into a dynamic revelation of who you really are and *why* you are here.

What Ripples Are You Making in the World?

Earth is a living consciousness, and is not inanimate. The earth is a life form, and everything upon this earth is a part of its life.

Earth is under an extraordinary expansion and is now shifting in alignment. This has an effect upon the form. However, know this: The reconfiguring is not an indicator of closure or total destruction. Rather, it is a sign of the living presence of the earth.

As the earth reshapes its form, and the forces that comprise this conscious being are forcefully present, this dynamically affects the critical nature of human life, too, as humanity is also going through an expansion.

This unexpected expansion of humanity is very much the infusion of a stronger heart-consciousness. The conflicts in the various nations are an awakening cry, the anguish of prying free from old selfish dispositions, the surrender of ideas that have battered humanity from the beginning.

In this hour, humanity is shattering the old feelings of disconnection. We are holding ourselves up to a standard of compassion and involvement.

When looking at the anger in the world, realize it is a force that moves lands and hearts. Anger, directed—with a clear desire to free the world's populations of harm and hatred—is a force for change.

In the populations that are forced to carry burdens for others, anger is the refusal to do so. It is a torch of personal sanctity, a fuel toward dynamic reprisal.

Life is the right to hold others up, not put them down. When we are able to feel *why* it is our task in life to lift up those who are burdened, that is when we feel the reason we exist.

Yes, hardship befalls many. But difficulties show us, remind us, and help us to *feel* why it is necessary to live for all, not only for ourselves. Our choices, with a reverence for all life, not only give *us* a deep calming ... but also ripple out around us, endlessly. It is then that we become a bearer of kindness, even if struggling through our own despair or fear.

The reservoir of hope and equanimity, calm and clarity, is found in the deepest, calmest place there is, inside of us.

Stop ... Be still ... Breathe ...

Be still ... Be still ... Be still ...

Feel and allow the pervading resonance...

What You Were Born to Do

That spark inside of you touches off in you an electric vibration of magnificence. *That* is who you are.

Your deepest driving force toward good spurs you. *That* is why you are here. To embody it.

All else is merely to help you focus it, define it, bring it into form. All else is life's way of showing you that you *do* know what to do and that you *can* do it.

Be the spark that is *your* dream. For it is up to you to make it real.

Say to yourself "*I am*" and your inner Light will grow and grow, and *you* will be a life force that helps to heal life's troubles.

How You Can Know the Right Path

No matter how much we think we know, there is no end to our capabilities and our potential.

To *know* the right path for you, daily be in the quiet soulful *stillness* and breathe in the divine calm. In that soft inner silence, release and judge not yourself. Judge not your choices. Only *feel* the serenity ... that is already there, deep inside you.

Be within the serenity. Breathe it in. This is home.

The answers will come.

How can you know the right choice?

Choose peace. Peace frees the heart. And a heart that is light in hope is a heart that lifts others up, and this is who you really are. One who helps others.

The vision you hold within is real.

It takes commitment. It takes a sense of purpose. Every day is the journey.

Life Is Calling You

When you expand your hope and allow your Dream, the creative consciousness then actively generates through you.

Every moment in life is an opportunity to open your entire Thought to whatever is within your reach, the cosmos around and within you.

When you open your Thought to the most unimaginable concepts, you are opening your ability to stretch in thinking, in ideas, and in solutions.

The world is a construct of Imagined Ideas. Everything around us, invented, was first *imagined*. That is the step to healing social issues, health issues, political issues, even relationship issues.

The world is a construct of Ideas manifest. Your task is to bring your Dream into form.

You chose this lifetime—to expand who and what you are, to fully express the Ideas borne in and through you.

Be the creator burgeoning from within.

Life is calling you.

The I AM to You

"*Be still and know that I am God* ... and I am with you in all matters of your life.

"I am with you through your open heart.

"I am with you as a Force of thoughtfulness and gratitude.

"I am in your disposition of tolerance.

"I am in your desire to be whole in your heart and mind.

"I am in your reasonable efforts to lift up any others who are downtrodden and feel lost.

"I am your sweet flowering into the full potential of your inner spiritual Nature.

"I am in your fully devout serenity amidst this world of both blessings and challenges.

"I am you when you are a bright spark of leadership.

"I am you as you give forth all that you are and can be to others who are in sorrow or despair.

"I am you through your goodness in both aspirations and travails. I am you whenever you hope to be a force that lifts up any others who seek solace.

"I am you in your best moments, and in your worst.

"*You* are the breath of all that is holy.

"*You* are the freshness of all that is divine.

"*You* are the being of all life. It is you. *You* are the Force of all life.

"I am all your hopes. I am that part of you that sings, that holds all others in regard, that is always beneficial in all matters. I am the part in you that sees hope in all people, in *all* creatures on this earth and in its waters, even on the earth itself.

"*You* are my enlightenment, humanity. *You* are the vision foreseen. *You* are the voices of the angels that surround you.

"We are all a Force. Let us sing with gratitude. In this, we are one.

"The I AM."

Revealed Teachings

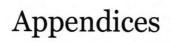

Appendices

A Vision

March 5, 1982 during seven-planet alignment

A delicate fragrance of rose potpourri filled my quiet room. I curled beneath my periwinkle-blue afghan and gazed out the bay window at the prisms of afternoon snow filling the crisp Colorado air, floating down softly and blanketing the earth white. The resonant dancing lights reached into my soul and embraced me.

Alive. I am. Forever.

In that moment, I could see beyond all boundaries, through all, and familiar thoughts streamed into my mind:

Be still. Be still and know that God is in you. Be still.

This mantra into my mind soothed me, calmed me, stroked away my fears.

Be still. Be still and know that God is in you. Be still.

Drowsiness overcame me and I drifted into a light nap, wherein I saw an iridescent figure. The familiar light-being took my hand, and warmth flowed through me. We lifted beyond this world to a very bright hall and stood before a large double door. It opened and we entered a lovely garden of flowers, with singing birds and flowing fountains.

The light-being departed and a tall, ageless, spiritual master walked toward me. His stride implied an inner strength born from much experience. Yet he came without grandeur, with a clear and steady gentleness. His brown hair and beard complemented his modest, brown priest's robe with a hood, of the ancient archetypal order of Melchizedek.

This handsome man, looking to be in his forties, came to me like a father. He came to me as a friend. His deep, brown eyes revealed a quiet and mellow nature.

"My name is Samuel," he said.

He took my hand and we strolled through the garden, as he explained that in one lifetime he had been known as the prophet Samuel in the biblical Old Testament. After many lifetimes and inner explorations, he had grown beyond the boundaries of external reality and the struggles of human life. No longer bound to a body, he had ascended as his true Self into the timeless realms as one of the Unseen, now neither masculine nor feminine.

That was when he remembered he was an oversoul—*my* oversoul, the being from whom I first came to exist as an independent personality.

Until age thirty, I had journeyed throughout my life without consciously knowing of my oversoul's existence. Yet Samuel had guided me. His feelings had impressed me; and his thoughts had reached into my deepest self, embodying the soul presence into my life.

Samuel and I now came to a room of mirrors. "Why have you come?" he asked me.

"I want to know," I answered humbly.

"What do you want to know?"

"Whatever you will show me."

We walked through the room, looking at my own many reflections of different incarnations, and Samuel said of other Ascended Masters, angels, and himself, "We have little more knowing than you, but we have come far since physical life. Perhaps our insights and understanding will help you and your friends find an easier way."

"What can I do?" I asked.

"Give. That is all we ask. Let others know that life is not coming to any end. Let them know that they are each a divine aspect of the universal life force. Let them know that beings exist who respect and love them and offer support on request. Let them know all that we will tell you. Be our messenger. Let us teach through you."

We returned to the garden and, as Samuel departed, a tall slender woman with long midnight-black hair approached me. She gazed at me warmly with love and affection, and a reverence fell over me. Alexandra was the other half of me, my "twin flame," who also originally had come from the same oversoul; then she and I had decided to explore different kinds of reality as separate selves.

"My gift," she said, "is to give you all you have known and to lift you up. Prepare yourself, my friend. Join me now."

We walked and I listened and learned, transcending into expanded visions and hope.

"Indeed," said Alexandra, "there is always hope."

She and I planned the rest of my current life and I came to remember what I had known before about the realms of limitless thought.

We then traversed the universes and I brought back memories of these sojourns, which I share in this and many other books.

"Embrace all, be all," said Alexandra. "Know that your dreams are already fulfilled, even as you give yourself to them."

The Seven

I was wakened out of a deep sleep at 4:40 a.m. May 7, 2011 with these words in my mind:

This is the I AM. I have a message.

I got up, went to my meditation room, and wrote down these words as they came into my mind, phrase by phrase:

"This is the I AM. Humanity, we in Life's Purpose hear you.

"Who are we that speak in the familiar language of soul through this teacher? We are Soul. We are Presence. The seven light sources that speak are in the direct line of the Alice Bailey tradition. We are the line of Melchizedek, the monastic Order of Knowledge. We are the revealers of Life's Purpose. We are seven, in service to all humanity and all life.

"Our purpose is clarity. Our purpose is teaching the inner way. We are seven of the soul of this teacher, whose being is tempered to the realms of the Divine Presence; whose life force is immersed in bringing insight regarding all the events shaping a new transcending and sweeping, lasting reinventing of the human nature.

"We are known as angels. The Divine is all. Our words are in the language of the Divine. We bear that Fullness as a lamp, to show what is coming. We speak from the fire of creation, which is ongoing and never ending. We cannot hold up any who fears. We are through with fear. We are now bringing words to fuel a true knowledge:

"Life is always. Life is never ending. Life is the wherewithal to hear simplicity. Life is not drudgery. In your own center is the answer to *all* questions.

"It is our task, with this teacher, to show the energy thoughts underpinning this world. It is our task, with this teacher, to focus why these new pressures are pushing out all old faded delusions of

Purpose. It is our task, with this teacher, to heal the uncertainty and to foster a more true Picture of what is in store for all in this world.

"We of this teacher's tempered light now open the doorway to Earth's evolution. This is not the end. Time does not end. Humanity does not end. Nature is not ended. Earth is now, already, vibrating to a pitch that cannot be stopped or avoided. All is now moving Purpose up to a view of the possible.

"Your being is light. You are *light*. The one truth is: All life is this essential element. Light is life. It is the visible Identity. It is an eternal driving power. It is your own vision, inside you. Inside your mind, light is the illumination, a magnetic essential component ... of all that lives. Illumination is life, its nature.

"Why do we say this now, we seven of the soul of this teacher? Because all you have thought is now *expanding*. Nothing will be as it was. All of the fears are only a need to see. See what? Your own inner essence—which is boundless illumination, unlimited ability to imagine, incredible cognizance to know all around you. Believe it. It is real.

"The I AM Presence (speaking) is the Fullness of this teacher. This teacher is tempered in these four attributes:

Listen to your knowing that guides you.

Live with the attitude that every being is the divine in body.

Open your mind to greater things than ever imagined before ... and they will become.

Live in hope ... because hope is the Divine guiding you.

"This teacher is of The Old Ones and is our human representative, conveying our words and ideas. With this teacher, we are able to help all of humanity begin to come out of the long slumber.

"We seven *are* the I AM life force. We serve only the good. We are the ancestors of this teacher. We are those who live to serve the Divine.

"*Breathe...*

"All is the Divine. All is in the Wisdom. And so it is."

From The Seven, September 15, 2011:

"We seven are from the Divine Alliance called the Angels of Serendipity.[9] It is our task, through this teacher, to share Insight— because humanity is awakening. The human race, on Earth and elsewhere, is now in its new strain.

"This is your time. You have awaited the Origin's arrival. You have anticipated the King's presence. You have requested the personal Elevation to touch you. You have held in your hopes that God is a pure and good Overseer.

"God is not an entity. God is the Presence of *All That Is,* that which is the vibrant essential quality that constructs elements, that called the Original Matter and the Quintessential Organic Substance and also the very qualities *From Which life* gestates.

"So, we seven are original Selves out of the Conscious Expansion. We have been since *The Thought* expanded out of the Essential Vortex.

"Now we can consciously tell you: You also came out of *The Thought,* and your new life is the example you have breathed in order to re-find your Original Definition.

"*Know this:* As a human, you are the example of *The Thought,* which sent Itself out To Be. You, now, are escalating ... through enhanced neuro links. You, now, can hear Thought guide you, teach you, and even heal you.

"We are the reminders. We remind you of who you are. We remind you how to hear us. We are all of The *Thought.* You, too, have

---

9 For more on this, read appendix "The Angels Today."

essential Supporters who guide you back to remembering. Your life is, now, about to expand—so that *your* voice is heard.

"Life is a place to be fully all that you are, in the serenity that is you. Invite that serenity. Tap it. Live it. It is *your* essential Self."

April 13, 2012 at the end of that morning's meditation:

I was expressing gratitude to the Source of these writings for the nurturing energy, when this inner response came to me:

"We are your Soul Council, seven who assist in this global awakening of all humanity, to help ease this first-ever shift into the physical dimension called *Full Presence*. It is our way of contributing to the whole, reminding everyone that *all* peoples have this same gift. It is who we all are. Everyone is able to access the *Full Mind.* "

Prophecies

The increasing intensity of earth's shifting and swaying is not to be feared. This will pass. Although the earth changes will continue for some time yet, they will pass.[10]

We are encouraged to remain tranquil. Although this passage may seem unrelenting, we are encouraged to be strong in discipline and persistent in obedience to our spirit. We are asked to help all who need us.

Earth Change Transitions Now Taking Place

The elements of the planet are crazy cockeyed. However, there is a degree of flexibility as to how severe this will be. It is possible to leash these powers that could destroy the planet ... but will not; they will only change it.

There are people on the planet who understand how to control these natural forces. This is being done, and their knowledge will make a difference.

A new lay of the land is expected. Lands will take new positions.

There will be a loss of power for a while, but stability will resume.

There will *not* be endless and absolute destruction of the planet. Earth will not end.

Symptoms of a Changing Earth

Fires and desolation — Upheavals and roaring fires, inside the planet and out. The planet is "swallowed in a sweeping fire of the

---

10 Received May 1982-1984

elements and purified through high technological destruction." (not a nuclear holocaust.)

Earthquakes — Shifting, shoving, pulling, breaching. Crusted elements break apart, down, over, up; shift, breathe, sigh. This is not in all areas on the planet, but in many. On average, this brings enormous failure of crops for a long time; therefore, food needs to be preserved and stored for emergency rations.

Sound waves — Shaking and shattering us and the earth. Many physical bodies, homes and landscapes are no longer safe from the destructive force of sound that comes from the ethers. It is not human-made, but from a *falling star* coming past us, shifting and shearing in our planet's pathway, a vibration that disassembles and breaks down [received December 1984].

Volcanoes — Even the greatest cities; flooding and sweeping through the masses.

Floods — High levels of water shoving overland from uprising lands in the oceans. The oceans are then re-dispersed. Where previously there were lowlands, below sea level and up to 500 feet, there will be marshes and lakes. Water displaces land in many places; the land is redistributed and rearranged. New systems of water control will be built later.

Thunderstorms — Temperatures clash, rising high, dropping low. The vestiges of this are powerful. Earthquakes with storms; the storms are enormous.

New Energy Source

We may attract the vibration of life from the ether. *Ether is a source of energy.* Ether is limitless and cannot be diminished. *Ether power* is beyond anything we have considered a form of natural law. *An accumulator of ether power* can fuel transportation and utilities.

Ether power may be used for regenerating tissue (healing bodies); in concept, we are not far from the ability to regenerate a previously destructive pattern of energy into a common good for recovery.[11]

Leashing the Forces of Nature

During this time of weather and earth changes, we can learn to transmute nature's effects. We can contain and redirect the forces of nature. We can leash the energy and control it through *an adapter of high magnetic life function that draws upon the energy frequency as it magnetizes in the ether, pulling the energy out of the ethers into a conductive material,* redirecting the force for good.[12]

How to Remain Safe

Earth changes are a consequence of energy patterns. Although enhanced by negative attitudes and emotions, earth changes are a natural evolution. The law of nature is supreme over all conditions on the planet. Nature is in some degrees a loving force: gentle rain of cleansing waters, rainbows, the transformation of barren land into blossoming green and flowers.

Although the power of natural law is unrestrained, we need not accept defeat in the face of the onslaught of these powerful forces; such as the earth spewing and shoving and turning about as a child in the womb about to birth, or the planet's cold and frigid areas melting and boiling and flooding the lands beneath it, or the temperate become milder and the mild becoming cold and the cold melting. All of these are a rhythm, a pattern evolving.

---

11 " New Energy Source" and "Leashing the Forces of Nature" received May 1982-83.

12 For additional and new prophecies and predictions, read book two of "The New Humanity" series, *The New Humans* (2017).

There will not be total demolition of the planet, but it is wise to be prepared. It is not enough to say, "I will be supported. I know my safety is determined."

Here are a few simple techniques of basic survival:

Lay aside a store of protective gear, safety equipment, and food rations for a period of five weeks to two years.

Even if the earth changes do not affect you personally, you can help others.[13]

---

[13] For extensive information on this topic, and also how to be safe from tornado, flash flood, forest fire, hurricane, and to find a lost dog—read my workbook *Intuition for Every Day*.

The Spiritual Meaning of *9/11*

The following uplifting and heartening message, received September 14, 2001, is applicable more so today than ever before.

Early on that Friday morning, before the national memorial service for the thousands of people who died at the World Trade Center in New York City, the U.S. Pentagon in Washington, D.C., and on the fields of Pennsylvania by those who heroically gave their lives, my heart cried out with the heavy weight of humanity's anguish and fear.

I went into a deep meditation seeking union with spirit and feeling a heartfelt desire to be of help in some way. The following words came *into* my mind ... to be shared with all, to offer us peace and assurance regarding the tragic events of *9/11,* September 11, 2001.

"*This* is the beginning of the new age. *This* is the threshold. *This* is the global initiation into the new age.

"This is the I AM. I bring renewal to all. This change is not only for the few. This is the new birth for all of humanity. The door is open. The way is clear. The darkness is behind you. You are walking into the light. Open your hearts and minds with belief in the goodwill of all.

"The Lord your God, by whatever name you know this Presence, is now in all hearts of the world—even those who have caused this suffering. Even in their blindness, they shall find the truth, for no heart is untouched by the grief felt around the world. No heart is able to hide from the illumination of the sorrow felt in every household.

"All over this world now, anguish rules. Causes are not above the need for coming together. Causes are now seen in perspective of the greater good for the whole of all peoples. The greater good leads the way now.

"From this point forward, as humanity comes into its new self-knowing, the desires of the world will be unity. However long it takes to heal the past—all past—however long it takes to join hearts and minds and purposes, this is a new era.

"Be not afraid. This is a time of renewal. Put your faith in living to your highest potential. That is where your peace lies. Focus your moments in living from your heart, wherein is your peace, your faith, and your hope.

"And so it is. The I AM.

"This is a new era. It is time to listen. Oh, ye of faith, believe in the Lord your God. Open the door to the light of retribution in a mind of truth in sight and vision of the will of God, which is: Love those who harm you. Forgive those who threaten you. Carry not hostile hearts. Carry not anger. Carry not despair. Carry faith in goodwill. Carry faith in creative force. Carry illumination to the four corners of the earth.

"Wisdom is the bearer of contemplation. Wisdom is born from hearts of an open and fresh desire to restore harmony. Wisdom is born from the creative force that lifts out of the ashes, illuminates faith and inspires purpose—not to avenge but to restore and build goodness in the world. Wisdom is a reflection of the desire to kindle justice.

"What is justice? Justice is a kind yet forceful persuasion that rekindles balance, that restores habit in the hearts of those who are blind, that re-establishes belief in fair and equitable treatment toward all living beings. Justice, in this case, is formed out of crisis and destruction. Yet the harmony is the babe of society.

"Crisis is the cries of an awareness to hold firmly together. Crisis is the awareness of the whole to believe together. Crisis is the womb opening and spilling forth the waters of new life. Crisis is the release of the ages of restraint. Crisis is the cusp of bringing a light into the darkness of what was, of light entering the world.

"Just as a child comes into the world, crying, so does the new vision, the new understanding. The new selves of the world's peoples now cry out: 'God! God of our fathers! God of our hearts! Hear us! Hear us, oh God, in whom we trust. God, hear us, send us your angels from heaven. God, in whom we seek to find understanding, believe in us. Give us wisdom. Give us hearts of knowing and reason. God of our fathers, help us in this hour to feel your hand upon us, that we may move softly. Help us to know not wrath but steadfastness. Dear Father, help us to believe in good. Help us to know that good prevails. Help us to have hearts of kindness.'

"My children, know this. This will pass. Just as a child is born, crying and thrashing and knowing not the light of the new world it enters, afraid and unsure of the new sounds and sights; just as a newborn infant comes into the world, so come you now into my arms, and feel my breath, and see my face, and hear the thunder of recognition, thunder to your ears because you have not before heard it, blinding light to your eyes because you have not before seen it. Now come you, my people, into a world of new experiences, new visions, new understanding. Now come you into a greater acceptance of each other than you have ever known.

"Just as a newborn infant must grow and learn, so do you, my children. Know this, I feel your pain, I feel your fear, I feel your thrashing against the uncertainties of this time. I am with you. I am always with you. Be not afraid.

"Your father in heaven, that which you call Allah, that which you call Goddess, that which you call Jesus the Christ, that which you call Buddha, that which you call Krishna, that which you call the Omnipotent, that which you call the I AM, I am with you all. By whatever name you know me, I am in your heart. My voice is the small truth that whispers within you—softly, with lamentation not.

"I speak not to rush you to unspeakable horrors. I speak to entrust you with compassion as you step forward to effectively heal the world of its ailing and vengeful souls. I speak to remind you that this is a time of action; it is a time to restore (to set anew) a foundation around the world: of peace, to eliminate discord, to create camaraderie among all souls, to bring to justice those souls who are blind and lack wisdom.

"Be not unkind in your hearts. Visit truth upon them not with retribution. Bring them to justice not out of rage. But let the decisive actions be as angels of mercy. Angels walk with you, among you, angels you see, angels you do not see. Walk as angels—with kindness, yet formidable to root out that which is not in accord with the whole.

"My children, from this day forth, whatever you see, whatever transpires, believe in the spirit of knowing kindness, act in the spirit of kindness. Let all you say and do be out of a desire to heal and bring comfort. And in this will you find the enemy, in this will you eliminate hatred—wherever it resides.

"God be with you all. Angels walk wit*h you and beside you. Angels abound around you, each of you. Open your eyes and your hearts. Therein is your mercy. Therein is your courage. Therein is your understanding.

"This is a great opportunity to eradicate cruelty. This is a *step* to breathe unity and to become one.

"This is a time of cleansing. This is a time of finding souls out of the rubble. This is a time of trust. This is a time of critical awakening. Souls of my heart, souls of my being, know that I am with you all—in every moment. You are not alone.

"Have faith. The crisis will pass. Peace will come. The peace you have believed. The peace you have hoped. The peace you have sought. This is the beginning.

"This is a time of renewal. This is a time to have faith—in God, in yourselves, in peace, in kindness. In this will you know safety. In this will safety find you. In this will good things come to you.

"This is a time of resolve. This is a time of resolution. This is a time of courage. Let your hearts be full. Sing praises unto your God. Ask forgiveness of your own judgments. And *know* that it is so. As you live, so shall you be. As you are, so shall you live. It has always been so. It shall always be so.

"This is a time of forgiveness—of yourself, your family, your friends, and also those who have hurt you. To be in the new life, open your heart, feel your pain, and *know* that this *will* pass. Not merely once again will you know peace. *That* was only in part. Now you will come to know peace in full measure—in your own heart, in your world. In that will you know that the ways of the world have changed forever. See before you now—as the sun rises—it *truly* is a new dawn for all of humanity.

"This is a time of reconstruction. This is a time of trust—in the powers that be, in government leaders, in religious leaders, in the rescuers, in the homeless, in the lost, in yourself. This is a time of faith—in all that your heart tells you is right, is good, is just, is fair. This is a time to know all *will* be well.

"This is the age of *knowing*. This is the age of *being*. This is the age of personal sanctity. This is the age of unfolding serenity. In this time is the rose breaking through the ground into the light. In this time is the first sight of blessedness. In this time is the first tear of recognition that all are truly of one heart, one breath, one body. In this time shall the world feel its heart, its center, and *know* that despite all sorrow, despite all fear, despite all anger: also there is a union of minds, a union that transcends the past, a union being born that will carry all forward in a light of common good and cheerful compassion; a light of courage and hope, a light of splendid purpose and insight. For all that has been is now in its last throes. All that has been is moving beyond its grasp. All that has been will fade away. Stand in your knowing heart. Therein is peace.

"THE I AM THAT I AM. Blessed be all who walk the earth. Blessed be all who reach out to each other. Blessed be all."

More About the Author

Charol Messenger spontaneously awakened to the universal consciousness at two a.m. November 2, 1975. As a result of this mystical activation, she has the spiritual gifts of clearly hearing, discerning, and interpreting the language of the soul—the "language of light."

Charol is a translator of esoteric knowledge and the etheric Akashic Records into human language in practical, everyday terms. All of the phases of her spiritual development that followed the awakening came upon her unbidden consciously and without any preparation or training; nevertheless, each phase was a part of the greater Soul Plan for this incarnation.

Carrying the signature and blueprint of her oversoul—the biblical prophet Samuel—Charol "elected" to be born in July 1945, between VE Day and VJ Day at the end of World War II, to be part of the upcoming transformative social changes on planet Earth.

In the fall of 1975, Charol encountered a life-threatening situation over several weeks. During highly charged and shattering encounters with dark spirits, she faced the "dark night of the soul." Latent psychic abilities and spiritual sight flooded to the surface of her consciousness, saving her physical life and her sanity. Thrust into dire circumstances and bombarded in her mind by images and tauntings by demons, she turned to prayer for the first time in fifteen years and asked God for guidance and protection. With the wisdom and strength of an old soul, she stood against the forces of darkness, stubbornly standing in the light and refusing to give in.

At the culmination of this "long dark night of the soul," Charol saw and heard the chorus of angels in heaven, and their ethereal light illuminated her bedroom during an *overlighting* by her oversoul consciousness. The outcome of this ordeal was the beginning of merging that higher consciousness into the physical body, mind, and personality.

This "soul merge," known esoterically as the Third Initiation, took six-and-a-half years to fully integrate. From five days before, through five days after March 5, 1982 (the day of a seven-planet alignment), this oversoul integration completed spontaneously, evidenced by eleven days of continuous heightened awareness and euphoria during which the oversoul consciousness fully embodied.

Two months later, in May, Charol was wakened out of a deep sleep by a gentle inner voice speaking *into* her mind, the voice of an angel on her soul council. This was the beginning of a writing phase during which Charol received, through inner dictation, several books from the oversoul consciousness on the spiritual path, the history and origin of the angels and how they help humanity, and our evolving human society. Charol received these books one at a time, taking dictation from the clear inner voice between the hours of two and four a.m., when she was wakened out of a deep sleep each night by an inner prodding. As she heard each word or phrase, she repeated it into a tape recorder. For the next twelve years, Charol transcribed, light edited, and integrated the information at a deep level of the Self. She did not publish these works; she only shared portions of the early pages with workshop participants as handouts, and with close friends.[14]

---

14 In addition to oversoul, senders of the 1982 portions of this book on how time and matter manifest in fourth-dimension physical reality were Alexandra and Josiah on Charol's soul council (described in *Wings of Light* and *You 2.0*). Alexandra also wrote the 1982 portions on mind and its functions regarding fourth-dimension consciousness and the fourth-dimension human body. Alexandra is part of Charol's same oversoul, from the same *original* spark of soul, and is currently a higher-dimensional being. Alexandra and Charol's first incarnation is relayed in *The Memory* (in revision). In addition to being the *muse* behind all of the Messenger books, Alexandra wrote *You 2.0* vol. I on Higher Self initiation and integration (workshop handout in 1987 was titled "The Daily Routine of a Developing Initiate"). (Other early pages handed out were "Higher Consciousness Workbook" the early development of the completed *Intuition for Every Day* and "Visions of Serendipity" the early draft of soon-to-be-published *Angels of Serendipity*.)

Then in 1994 another spontaneous event occurred during a six-month 24/7 period of exalted consciousness that resulted from very deep and prolonged meditative states, two hours at a time, daily. Having left a full-time job in April, Charol spent 100 percent of her time committed to renewing the connection with her spiritual Self, and she thrived on the rejuvenation.

After seven weeks, during an especially deep meditation, Charol *lifted* to a place in higher consciousness she had never reached before (and didn't know she could, had not sought it nor expected it). Writing from this new pristine place within the soul—the most pure place one can reach and bring back the insights into the world— Charol wrote four new books within four months, and a fifth soon after. She spent all of her waking hours transcribing (and absorbing) the inner-dictated materials; which, interestingly, she now received in her own point of view as if she had sat down and written them, including the anecdotes about her own life, which she had never before consciously realized.

Into these five books from the Higher Mind, the same essential ideas and topics were conveyed as had been received twelve years previously, except now in new words and with flawless writing: the angels in our everyday lives *(Wings of Light* and *Walking with Angels),* the spiritual path and our eternal soul journey *(The Soul Path),* humanity's first incarnation *(The Memory),* and the origins and evolution of humanity *(The New Humanity,* 1st Ed., which is Vol. I in the 2012 updated and expanded *Humanity 2.0;* the original *New Humanity* concept draft was received in 1982, then re-received spontaneously in 1994, as you see it).

The revelations, mystical knowledge, and prophecies in all of these books are written in the Higher Mind, through the oversoul consciousness. All of the books are published verbatim as received, word for word; except for light editing, renaming and rearranging some chapters, and adding subheadings.

As a futurist and global visionary, awakened to cosmic consciousness and her oversoul in 1975, then the I AM Consciousness in 1994, Charol is a *spiritual revealer,* attuned to the undercurrent hum sweeping through humanity today. She is revealing humanity's long foretold evolutionary transformation—that is happening *right now.*

Humanity is in *transcension.* We are in it, now.

Being Within the Oneness

UCCS world-religions paper 1985-87
by Charol Messenger

"We need to be reminded of our common universal heritage... [That] we are really One." ~ Hasting Moore

Most of us view a fragment of the whole. We perceive that fragment as our personal experience. But we are seeing only one piece of the puzzle of reality.

In this age of transition, humanity is beginning to grasp that we have been viewing and experiencing only a fragment of reality. We are becoming aware that we are not separate and independent, but that we are one with all of life. That to flow with this oneness reduces the stress of our feeling alienated. That to flow with the whole and allow ourselves to interact is to perceive that we are all equal. We are one. We are one because everything needs something else in order to exist.

In 1902, American philosopher William James wrote in his *Varieties of Religious Experience,* "Our normal waking consciousness, rational consciousness as we call it, is but one special type of consciousness, whilst all about it, parted by [only] the flimsiest of screens, there lie potential forms of consciousness entirely different."

Seventeenth-century French philosopher Rene Descartes tells us, in the preface to his meditations, "Meditate seriously along with me... Be capable of freeing the mind from attachment to the sense, and clearing it entirely of all sorts of prejudices." Descartes tells us to contemplate within self, rather than to look to external sources for our answers and guidance. And that, although processing and using what we learn is important, we do more truly gain wisdom through being still within and allowing cosmic consciousness (soul consciousness) to speak to us through our inner feelings, thoughts, and images.

"Even ordinary human beings," Descartes says, "if they would experience objects as given in perception, must stop thinking and simply perceive. To be inwardly convinced of their reality they must slacken the tension of the pure intellect and let themselves flow with the dream of sensuous experience."

Our clearest perceptions lie in the total awareness that is available to any who taps into the consciousness of soul.

> "Within the inner solitude there appears to be a consciousness transformation that takes place without any effort on the part of the individual in whom it is occurring.
>
> "'Let practice be the proof,' the *Cloud* (*of Unknowing*) assures the reader. 'This inner growth appears to occur, under appropriate conditions of receptivity, purely as an action originating in the Source itself.'" ~ Hastings Moore

Since 1975, I have been so able to so attune myself that I am able, at will, to allow fresh concepts to come clearly into the center of my awareness as empathic knowing, feelings, intuitive flashes, visual imagery, and/or in the symbols of thoughts and words.

Much as a radio receives music and words over channels, I attune my frequency/vibration to inwardly receive, which I do by entering an alpha state of consciousness. In this quietude, I hear the words spoken to me in my mind.

To receive clearly, I must be attuned, primarily in attitude: a sense of openness and allowing, nonjudgmental and willing to learn something new and unfamiliar. Self-honesty leads to knowing and self-discovery.

> "It must be done by means of forgetting and losing self-consciousness. It is in the stillness, in the silence, that the word of God is to be heard. There is no better avenue of

approach to this Word than through stillness, through silence. It is to be heard there as it is--in that unselfconsciousness, for when one is aware of nothing, that word is imparted to him [or her] and clearly revealed."

~ On Eckhart, - Hastings Moore

The Tao of Physics, Fritjof Capra

Golden Scripts, transcriptions by William Dudley Pelley; Aquila Press, Inc. or Fellowship Press, Inc., Noblesville, Indiana

The Power of Myth, Joseph Campbell, interviewed by Bill Moyers; video collection from Mystic Fire Video, P.O. Box 9323, Dept. RA, S. Burlington VT 95403; audio collection from New Dimensions Tapes, P.O. Box 410510, San Francisco, CA 94141

The Nature of Personal Reality, a Seth book, Jane Roberts

The Unobstructed Universe, Stewart Edward White

The I-Ching Workbook, R. L. Wing

The Neighborhood of Is, Approaches to the Inner Solitude, Hastings Moore and Gary W. Moore, University of Colorado at Colorado Springs, 1982

The Philosophy of Descartes, Alexander Boyce Gibson, Russell & Russell, 1932

The American Red Cross Emergency Test, P.O. Box 158, Orangeburg, New York 10962 (transcript of documentary, $2)

Holism: A New Trend in Humanity's Consciousness

Mind-Body Interaction, Elements of a Whole Self
A definition of soul

UCCS philosophy course thesis paper 1985-87
by Charol Messenger

This holistic philosophy on the elements of soul is based on a study of Rene Descartes' Cartesian dualism and supported by twentieth-century American philosopher John Dewey, as well as other noted philosophers. The quoted texts concur with my own philosophical statements. Both build a definition of soul....

Mind is primary matter, meaning it manifests that which is visible to the naked eye. Mind, or thought, is energy. As such, we can consider mind as a degree of matter. The degrees of mind and body are similar only in their core description, being composites of molecules, atoms, etc. It is their appearance that is distinct, not their content.

In view of this, it would seem that both mind and body—which are energy—may be constituted of what we think of as physical properties. Yet third dimension matter (body) is a manifestation of primary matter, which we do not see with physical eyes, which would be mind, but perhaps also spirit, or vital force, which seems to be an element not the same as mind. And this idea of spirit, or vital force, leads us into the next theme of seeing more distinctly the elements of a whole person.

It may be that what we call soul is actually the whole person, being composed of at least the elements of: mind as thought, spirit as vitality, and body as a manifestation and fulfillment of these. In *The Marriage of Heaven and Hell,* British poet William Blake says, "Man has no body distinct from his soul. For that called body is a portion of soul."

In my present degree of evolving consciousness, it is my philosophy that our body is a manifestation of our consciousness, that consciousness is the reality, the person, i.e. pure energy, which manifests in form, or body. Why? That is a whole other issue; but, briefly, it is to experience tactile sensation and interrelationships.

In speaking of bodies/forms as manifestations of our consciousness, I am not limiting this premise to my third-dimension existence in this present time-space life. I am also considering other lives I may experience in a physical embodiment (i.e., reincarnation or multidimensional realities). I am also considering the various degrees through which I as a self am evolving in self-awareness, i.e. consciousness. And it is this that is existence. I am not dependent on time-place to exist, but I exist as a conscious self-aware being who expresses itself through a form. Again, why? In order to experience the multi-facets of interaction with others in complex levels of reality, such as Earth.

No, we do not depend on our bodies for survival, but we do depend on them and integrate with them as vehicles to express our beingness.

How can body be an extension of mind? How can it be a manifestation of thought energy? How is this not strictly dualism?

Mind is thought is energy. Body is energy. These two energies differ only in their vibratory rate. The faster vibration (thought) is not visible and can influence the slower vibration (body) which is physical and visible. It can do so only because thought as energy is able to manifest into "matter" which is only more condensed energy because of its lower vibration.

Mind and body are both energy and substance. That which is merely energy becomes matter. That which is matter reverts to energy. Matter (body) is not the same degree or vibration as thought, but a different way of receiving that energy because of differing vibrations.

So we see that mind and body differ in their manifestations as energy, and they differ in their vibratory rate. Yet both are energy and can, therefore, influence one another. So we see that mind and body are the same though different.

Let us consider how mind and body are the same. In 610 B.C., Anaximander held that all things come from a single primal substance which is infinite, eternal, and ageless. Albert Einstein, in his equation $E = mc2$, restated the ancient concept of the equivalency of matter and energy. In other words, matter is energy.

Mind and body are energy. It is the rate of vibration that determines the degree of shape or essence. The vital force of our essence is also energy, and this vital force is called spirit. So it may be that our whole being is composed of mind, spirit, and body.

When I consider soul, I think of my whole essence. This is a holistic philosophy, also called system theory. When I choose to consider an element only, such as my flesh body and its function and operation, or my spirit and its vitality, or my mind and its thoughts, then I am studying what may be elements of my essence.

I would only study an element in order to better comprehend how it may affect or be affected by other element(s) or to the whole. We may observe our essence from any perspective. And the better we are able to study any of these aspects or the whole, then the better understanding we have of what it is to be healthy, happy individuals and how—although in a cosmic sense we are one with all life, which includes all individuals.

Plato, speaking for Socrates, says in *The Tripartite Structure of the Soul*, "The just man does not permit the several elements within him to interfere with one another... He sets in order his own inner life, and is his own master and his own law, and at peace with himself; and when he has bound together the three principles within him...the higher, lower, and middle... then he proceeds to act...always thinking and calling that which preserves and cooperates with this harmonious condition."

Mind is always connected to the body, but mind is not the body. Even outside of third dimension earth physical, we continue to wear forms or bodies of some nature: meaning that which can be weighed and measured, even though not contained or with perimeters such as we now have. This concept comes to me through deep level meditation. In view of supporting the idea of the body being an important possible element of soul, the probable fact that we have bodies in all existence—whether in this life on Earth or in other places and times and beyond that—supports this holistic idea.

Regarding the nature of our "body" as we evolve: We always have a body, or form; but our body changes from one plane of expression to another; i.e., the various life existences we may experience in assorted periods of time-space, including those that are outside of third dimension but are still a part of our individual expression. In all of these existences we have form (or body), but the form—although maybe similar throughout—does not in and of itself continue. We have form. But we are not our form, except that our form reflects the level of our evolution as pure energy, or light.

Following are two statements to support this thesis, keeping in mind that body, mind. and spirit are all energy and therefore the same, though of differing constitutions:

Now that we have reaffirmed that body is energy, as are mind and spirit, let us look at the elements more closely. This view is not to separate the parts but to show how they work together to a common end. This is supported by the twentieth-century American philosopher John Dewey.

Mind is the bridge between the spirit and the body. Mind is not the brain. Mind is an element of soul. Brain is an element of the body and is, therefore, the bridge between the mind and body. The brain is an instrument that unites the thought process of mind and its function in the body.

So that, we are seeing mind expressing its energy through the brain and into the body. And we see spirit vibrating through the entire system. Spirit is the vital force, possibly the electrical charge, and this brings to mind that which may work in the body itself through the nervous system.

This is not a complete formula, as yet, but is an initial insight into the possible way in which the various elements work together for the whole person. Primarily, I feel it is significant to keep in mind that I am merely construing how the elements of the whole may function together.

Let us look at the element of consciousness, whether it be the soul entirely, or only one of the elements. Consciousness is an ingredient that seems to pervade our whole essence, so it cannot be confined to the brain. Consciousness may be more than thought since it seems to encompass our feelings, so it is likely not mind alone either. And in some way consciousness seems synonymous with breath, which is our vital force; so perhaps breath is spirit, and perhaps spirit is also of this consciousness. It would seem plausible that the soul imbues our essence and matter—at whatever degree of vibration—with consciousness.

Consciousness seems to contain feelings, insight and awareness, as well as thought. Consciousness is more than thought. It is not confined to the mental. It seems to express our full awareness, or at least is capable of this. Let us suppose then that thoughts are expressions of spirit as well as mind, so we may find that consciousness is a facet of all elements rather than only one.

With this reasoning, consciousness may be the way of identifying soul itself. In fact, we can consider that even the body has its own level of consciousness—that which has its own memory and experience in the cells themselves. We see then that consciousness may be the motivating factor of our being—at all levels or degrees of development.

So, our formula may be: soul = consciousness; i.e., spirit, mind, matter. And if we use the term "thought" to denote consciousness, as is generally accepted, we find correlating theories to support this concept. Particularly, I refer you to *Space-Time and Beyond* by Toben and Wolf.

So, it is our thoughts that manifest in form. Or perhaps more correctly, it is our consciousness—not merely the words we think but also our reflexes, responses, attitudes, etc. So that, if we "think" positively, we manifest positively, such as in health. And if we "think" negatively, we manifest negatively, such as in illness. Our physical body (especially in its ongoing changing condition) is the manifestation of our "thoughts," or more precisely, our consciousness.

So I contend that all elements interact and affect one another.... How we view body and soul may be a question only of perception. We can see the body as destructible and material, and see the soul as nondestructible and immaterial; or we can take a holistic approach and see the soul as possibly composed of elements—integrated....

Plato reports, for Socrates, in *The Immortality of the Soul:* "When the soul and the body are united, then nature orders the soul to rule and govern, and the body to obey and serve."

REFERENCES

Amorc, Rosicrucian Digest, Mindquest: "Energy: Spirit of the Universe, Part I; The Unity of Matter and Energy" by Onslow H. Wilson, Ph.D., visiting scientist, Rose-Croix University; April 1979, p17-19.

Amorc, Rosicrucian Digest

Mindquest: "Energy: Spirit of the Universe, Part II; the Unity of Matter and Energy" by Onslow H. Wilson, Ph.D.

Bannan, John F., The Philosophy of Merleau-Ponty, Harcourt, Brace & World, Inc., 1967

Bradley, F.H., Appearance and Reality: A Metaphysical Essay, Clarendon Press, Oxford, 1893

Dewey, John, "Soul and Body," published in The Philosophy of the Body: Rejections of Cartesian Dualism, edited by Stuart F. Spicker, Quadrangle Books, 1970

Faraday, Dr. Ann, Dream Power, Berkeley Publishing Co., 1972

Levin, Michael E., Metaphysics and the Mind-Body Problem, Clarendon Press, Oxford, 1979

Phillips, D.C., Holistic Thought in Social Science, Stanford University Press, 1976

Slote, Michael A., Metaphysics and Essence, New York University Press, 1975

Stevenson, Leslie, The Study of Human Nature, Oxford University Press, 1981

Toben and Wolf, Space-Time and Beyond, in conversation with theoretical physicists, E.P. Dutton, NY, 1982.

Recommended
Movies, TV, Books, Audio, Video

First, I highly recommend *Networked Intelligence (Vernetzte Intelligenz)* by von Grazyna Fosar and Franz Bludorf, published 2001 in German, www.fosar-bludorf.com.

The following excerpt opens the discussion on how science is identifying greater capacities of the brain, including what have been considered extraordinary abilities, such as clairvoyance and telepathy—which I believe are innate within all human beings and will be evidenced more and more as humanity's evolutionary leap continues:

"New research suggests that human DNA is a virtual biological Internet and superior in many aspects to the artificial one. Could the latest Russian scientific findings help to explain the phenomena such as clairvoyance, intuition, spontaneous and remote acts of healing, self-healing, affirmation techniques, unusual light, auras, spiritual masters, the mind's influence on weather patterns, and much more? The answer may be yes.... Only 10% of our DNA is being used for building proteins.... The other 90% has been called 'junk DNA.'"

I also highly recommend:

2017 movie, *A Dog's Purpose,* based on the book *A Dog's Way Home* by w. Bruce Cameron

2016 movie, Marvel's *Dr. Strange*

2017 book, *Gifts from the Edge,* Claudia Watts Edge, a personal favorite, true insights and visions of life beyond death

In addition:

Hands of Light, Barbara Ann Brennan

Vision, Ken Carey, Harper San Francisco

Mastery Through Accomplishment, Hazrat Inayat Khan

Freedom in Exile: The Autobiography of the Dalai Lama

Surfing the Himalayas, Frederick Lenz

The Seat of the Soul, Gary Zukav

Living with Joy, Sanaya Roman

The Possible Human, Jean Houston

The Cultural Creatives, Paul H. Ray

Initiation, Elizabeth Haich

The Sacred Journey: You and Your Higher Self, Lazaris

Space-Time and Beyond, Toben and Wolf

Illusions, Jonathan Livingston Seagull, Richard Bach

The Education of Oversoul Seven, Jane Roberts

Psychic Self-Defense and Well-Being, Melita Denning and Osborne Phillips

The Impersonal Life, DeVorss & Co., Publishers

Life and Teaching of the Masters of the Far East, Baird T. Spalding

The Celestine Prophecy, James Redfield, Warner Books

"Getting in the Gap," Wayne Dyer

Pathways to Mastership, audio set, Jonathan Parker; Gateways Institute

"Chakra Balancing and Energizing" audio, Dick Sutphen

Joseph Campbell videos on mythology

I have not read the following books, so as not to influence my own writings, but I recommend them based on their topics, for a broad view of what visionaries are sharing.

The Third Millennium, Ken Carey, Harper San Francisco

The Power of Now, The New Earth, Eckhart Tolle

Bashar: Blueprint for change, Darryl Anka, New Solutions Publishing

New Cells, New Bodies, New Life! Virginia Essene, S.E.E. Publishing

You Are Becoming a Galactic Human, Virginia Essene and Sheldon Nidle

Made in the USA
San Bernardino, CA
26 February 2019